MY STRAWBERRY HILL

By

JOANNA KLEE SHIVELY

Joanna Klee Shively

About the cover: Mrs. Shively won a blue ribbon in 2002 from the Ozark Piecemakers Quilt Guild for the quilt which appears on the cover of this book.

ISBN: 1-58597-193-6

Library of Congress Control Number: 2003107266

A division of Squire Publishers, Inc.
4500 College Blvd.
Leawood, KS 66211
1/888/888-7696
www.leatherspublishing.com

FOREWORD

I will be 99 years old on July 21, 2003.

While I can still hold a pen, I am going to write my biography for my descendants, thereby helping them as I enlighten them about me and our "family tree." I do not want Roget or Webster close by to help with big, seldom-used words. I will use simple words to relate day-to-day history, some comical, some not so comical, and some intensely tragic. I want to imagine the faces of my dear ones around me, as I tell from research and memory about the large family of Knauers, of which we are the branches. At this point in time, we cannot easily learn how far back in years the Knauers existed, as records were not kept as precisely as today for most of us. Our oldest records are dated 1560.

The wealthy, famous and even infamous are preferred subjects for biographers. Seldom do the in-between, "tend to your own business" folks draw their attention, although we outnumber all the rest. There are millions of unsung average Americans, eager to leave to posterity their legacy of good character, citizenship, patriotism and varied experiences for those to come.

With few exceptions, the following pages contain the story of my life. Though written especially for my children, it will no doubt reflect on the lives of some American families.

After a great deal of research by my granddaughter, Reneé Carter Lichtman, use of the Internet, etc., I have learned much more than I had hoped for, considering the passing on of generations on several continents. Another granddaughter, Julie Carter Foth, is handling the legal matters of which I know nothing, and my daughter, Sally Dyer, has spent countless hours typing the material as I compose it. I have never been able to use the computer easily, as I did the old Underwoods, etc. Our friend, Charlyn Van Oosbree, a librarian, helped with the proofreading of my story.

I am grateful to everyone who contributed time and effort to this endeavor. Hopefully, some reader out there will recall something from his or her past that would tie in with the characters and events in this account, as I have learned that the Knauers are scattered all over the world, especially in the fields of writers, teachers, physicians and lawyers. First records found them to be farmers, vintners and public servants.

There is a mystery in the early part of my life which has never had a glimmer toward a solution — perhaps it will happen at this late date.

My family tree is dead and gone
I've heard folks sadly say,
But 'tis not true — no "trees" are dead
For we "branches" live today.

—*J.K.S.*

INTRODUCTION

Most of our ancestors came from one European country or another. My father's homeland was in the Hanover area in the northern part of Germany. I have very few particularly informative bits of his background, as he was not with us during our inquisitive years. His father farmed and also operated a mill with another son. He did his military service required by the government before coming to America. I have his honorable discharge papers found among my mother's keepsakes.

My mother's people came from Grünbach, a village near Stuttgart, Germany, near the beautiful Black Forest area, in the southern part of the country. Grünbach is hard to find on an average-sized map, but instructions for getting there are thus: By taking the train in Stuttgart and traveling up the lower valley of the Rems, after an hour's ride, you may see on the left, at the foot of the hills surrounded by vineyards, the idyllic village of Grünbach.

My family men were vintners, which are grape growers, wine makers, wine merchants and even dispensers. I can almost visualize the men coming in from the fields at the day's end to their three-storied homes. The large animals lived below the first floor of the family's quarters. The third floor with the hitch-pitched roof was occupied by the retired or infirm elders. The same space-saving dwellings may still be seen in the farming areas of Germany. This information comes from a friend who grew up in the Swabian section of Germany. Today we would all resent living in such close proximity to large animals. However, who can say what is ahead of us with the world's population reaching six billion in the last decade.

My trips to Germany have all been with bus tours, when schedules and points of interest have been pre-arranged. My choices would have been southern Germany, near the Black

Forest area, and precisely the city of Stuttgart and villages such as Nürtigan and the hamlet of Grünbach. This was my ancestors' homeland as far back as 1600. A Philadelphia cousin calls the area unbelievably charming.

Time and progress may have changed the contour of the land in and around Grünbach, but I like to dream about the little community when my family roots, the Knauers, were making their living as the seasons rolled around, sending their product for many generations to innumerable countries.

1

PAULINE ELIZABETH KNAUER KLEE, my mother, was born October 23rd, 1871, in Nurtingen, Germany, just a stone's throw from Stuttgart. This is the historic Swabian region of southern Germany which includes the beautiful Black Forest area. Grünbach, a mere hamlet near Nürtlingen, is the ancestral home town of the Knauer family.

My mother was the youngest of the six children, born in this order: Mary Katherine, Frederick, Carl, William, Sophia, and my mother, Pauline Elizabeth; they were about two years apart in age.

At about the age of one month, baby Pauline's mother was thrown from the carriage she was ascending. Apparently the horse became startled or frightened, causing a sudden jerk as it ran. The occupant's skirt may have wrapped around the hub of the wheel; who knows? The result was instant death according to bystanders, who no doubt were holding the luggage, or even the baby.

This mother of six young children was a very unhappy lady; it has been suggested that she was so mentally troubled that she may have planned the accident, hoping to die. I don't think so. Horse and vehicle accidents were not uncommon. Had she considered suicide, she would have taken another way out. The following letter to her minister indicates she was a devout Christian mother who would not break one of the commandments by deserting her young children and killing herself. Her letter was written in old German script. My researcher spent considerable time trying to locate someone who could transcribe it into English. My grandmother must have written this letter to her minister just after my mother Pauline was born, and shortly before she was killed in the accident. Apparently she was in a very confused state of mind as she wrote the following letter:

Dear Brother Wacker, (transcribed as written)

I cannot do without writing you a few words before I have to leave Stuttgart. I would like to have visited with you, but circumstances did interfere; because I can't stand the driving and walking is out of the question and all the worries of my crying have made me feel bad; and my Heavenly Father knows it. How many hours have I been here in Stuttgart, with my sorrow that I do not divulge to anybody. It is terribly hard to stand it, that I am so far away from believers, that believe the same as I. I can only go every Sunday to people who believe the same as I do.

This kind of living is not for me — drinking and gambling. I can hardly write about all these things. If it would not by myself, six children, I would leave everything behind (money and possessions) whatever it is she is forced to live this kind of life. I just cannot be happy anywhere, as long as I have to look at this life.

Dear Bro, I much better would go to graveyard than live with such a man. I have too often go to my Heavenly Father for help, "Dear Father, where do you want me to go? Do I always have to walk in these waters?" I cannot get any comfort except when I look heavenward to my dear Jesus. There is absolutely nobody here on earth that can help me. The only help for me is God's word, but it is hard for me — do not have the courage or the patience — like Job. I can get comfort from the Psalms.

Dear Bro Wacker, I often think about the many words we have talked about. At that time it was hard to leave Stuttgart — now it is even harder to go to strange people. Please keep me in your thoughts and in your prayers, and I will write to you. I will close this letter; say hello to all my sisters and brothers, and to you and your wife and Christian and his wife. Say hello in God's name. Think of me and visit me whenever possible. Dear Brother Wacker, I would pay gladly for your fare both ways. The town where I am going to Schlosshoff in Michelfield Hall. Yours in Jesus Christ and Believer.

Elizabeth Knauer

P.S. Maybe I will be next Sunday the last time in Stuttgart. I would have liked to have written to you in (Maisfingen) but I do not have time. I write to you when I am at my destination.

Author's Comment:

Whiskey makes the man a swiller,
It wrecks the mind and soul;
Better pitch that silent killer
And keep your body whole.

2

LITTLE PAULINE WAS FOND of her father, but no doubt his attention had to be divided scantily between her and five others aged about 2, 4, 6, 8 and 10. She told us that as she grew into school age, she and her father spent some happy times together; she especially liked the walks in the Black Forest area near their home. I believe he was as good a father as he could be and no doubt tried to give some extra time to his little girl who had barely experienced the feeling of her mother's arms. What a tragic affair for her! But she never dwelt on this inequity in her childhood, having had nothing to compare it with.

No one who lost their natural mother at the age of one month can ever know the feeling of bonding to another. Bare necessities were probably all the care Pauline was ever given.

I know my grandfather remarried very soon. With five other dependent children to tend, and the stepmother trying to "learn the ropes" of the household, there was little time left to give the tiny baby the special care it deserved.

To know that their mother was never coming back must have been nearly unbearable for the children. The two-year-old would soon forget and accept the new mother. Controlling the birth rate was unheard of in the 1870s, and the arrival of three more children in rapid succession was no surprise.

Unfortunately, Pauline did not get along well with the stepmother. Several of her siblings left the home while quite young, sailing to America with great eagerness for the good life and opportunities. It was natural that Pauline would have thoughts of trying for the better life also. With a promise that she would continue her education in America, Pauline, then just 14, and a girlfriend a bit older, left the homeland (I have the passenger list which was found many years later among her keepsakes and souvenirs).

Two of Pauline's sisters, Mary Katherine and Sophia, also two brothers, had preceded her in the great influx of immigrants to the United States in the late 1800s. So there were loved ones anxiously awaiting Pauline on Ellis Island's 27 acres. No doubt there were four sets of arms eager to embrace little sister.

My grandfather's children by second marriage were Emma, William and Christian. William's son became a lawyer in Philadelphia, Pa., and his wife, Virginia, was very prominent in President Nixon's administration. His sister, Emma, was in charge of his restored inn, later a museum known as "Man Full of Trouble," and a part of the Knauer Foundation in Philadelphia.

3

MY MOTHER WAS adept at many things. She had studied English, so the main language in America was no problem for her. She knew also more than a smattering of other European languages, due to close proximity to several countries, especially France, Austria and Switzerland that border on the south. She carried out her promise to her father to continue her education in America. I know there was considerable traveling to Europe over the years, but I think my mother and father went over only once.

As we all know only too well, few wage-earning opportunities were available to young ladies before the turn of the century. Teaching school was the preferred choice outside of the home. Pauline was a chaperone for children sometime in her twenties. She must have had, in addition to that, some training in nutrition and fancy food preparation, for she was an excellent cook and very knowledgeable about health food.

Mother was a very happy girl when she was young. She liked places that were "swinging" as some call it today. She liked dancing the waltzes and going to entertainment areas. Coney Island and Central Park were popular with the young, and no doubt much different and safer than today.

It is sad to think women had to wait so many years to prove that equality was definitely here, but ability to prove it was not given a chance. A much happier time could have been in the world for all of our predecessors. Women's natural innate knowledge about children, home, food and welfare is as important as the work in fields and factories. What good is production of food without the ability to put it into its intended use? The good guys of today realize the importance of women's child care and housekeeping, since most mothers are earning second checks to augment the style of living we enjoy in our time.

4

MY FATHER, JOHN Christoff Klee, was born on August 6, 1869; he was of northern German parentage. The city of his birth is Hanover, in Lotrum Province ("Klee" means clover in the German language).

How my parents met I do not know, only that it happened in America. My mother was very tight-lipped, telling her children only what she wanted them to know. She was very proud of her homeland in the south and described it for us often.

From bits of conversation, we children learned that our mother's choice of a husband was not approved of by her siblings.

Be that as it may, John Christoff Klee and Pauline Elizabeth Knauer were married on March 9, 1901, by The Reverend Kandelhart. It was witnessed by some friends, the Quickerts, and several relatives. I learned later that the exact place was Richmond Hill, on Long Island. I have the marriage record and the wedding photograph. Pauline was wearing a lovely taffeta dress and short veil. She also carried a bouquet of flowers, and artificial orange blossoms were scattered around in the veil. Father wore a formal suit. That seemed to be the proper attire for most weddings at that time.

They spent their honeymoon on a relative's farm, not far from the family. This was customary as traveling to distant spots was a difficult undertaking, except for the rich who would take a voyage of some kind.

From what I learned by listening to conversation here and there, the new wife's duty was to get acquainted with the kitchen where she would spend much of her life. I hope it is untrue that the husband-to-be had the right to have a meal cooked by his intended before he would propose marriage. I don't believe my father was so demanding, but if so, he would have jumped at the chance to propose, for Mother was an excellent cook.

Eating out had not come into fashion, except once again, for the rich, who employed a staff for cooking and serving and everything else. Makes one wonder what the wife did all day — perhaps that is when the game of bridge came into vogue!

5

PLANS WERE NOT made for children, when or how many there should be. They were an expected part of marriage, and usually a welcome addition, I feel sure. In many families, the interest was not just in what we could do for our children, but what they could do for the family; understandable when there was so much manual work to do. Of course, not all men were farmers, but almost all homes had gardens, fruit trees, chickens and a large animal or two, all of which made work and required many hands to do it.

In our family, there was a pregnancy soon after the marriage, but the little boy, Robert, miscarried. A second pregnancy happened soon after. On August 3, 1902, a daughter was born and named Mary Elizabeth for her mother and aunt, Mary Katherine (Von Lang), also living in New York. Elizabeth, as she was usually called, was a very frail child. (She could not attend school until seven years of age.) I came along next on July 21, 1904. They named me Maida Johanna. Maida is one of many variations of Margaret, as are similar names like Maggie, Peggy or Meg. When I was old enough to have a preference, I settled for Joanna.

Our family increased again with the premature birth of John Frederick on Christmas Eve, 1906. He weighed less than three pounds. He did survive, but was never well. Carl William was born July 16, 1908; he was an average healthy baby. Sister Caroline Louise was next — she lived only five months. There was one more premature brother. He was barely alive — lived a very short time. Doctors said, "Not much can be done for an unfinished baby." No doubt he could have survived if they had had the wonderful methods used today.

My poor mother, who wanted a large family, was very healthy—just couldn't carry her babies full term. My brother Bill and I were the only healthy ones of the seven pregnancies. Our brother John was never well physically and quite slow mentally, requiring much care and concern for our parents. From the time he was 18 months old, he had regular trips to doctors who administered various kinds of treatments. He walked quite well by his eighth birthday, but was unwell most of the time. School attendance was quite irregular all his life.

 6 

6

WE LEFT RICHMOND HILL when I was very small, perhaps three years old. Father liked the resort business and its many activities. He found it on the Pennsylvania side of the Delaware River, where Flatbrookville, New Jersey, was just across the river.

There is a place in Pennsylvania called "Krupp's Place." I can't tell you how to get there, for the face of the surrounding land has long since been lifted, leveled, terraced and dredged to invite the nearby river to create a small lake or two. I can just tell you that "Krupp's Place" is located on the west bank of the Delaware River, in Pike County, Pennsylvania, near the village of Bushkill, a little bit north of the Delaware Water Gap, the scenic wonder through the Kittatinny Mountains. "Krupp's Place" was our home.

My interest was not confined to the west bank, but continued across the river to New Jersey, and specifically to the little village of Flatbrookville, struggling to retain its flimsy hold to the base of the New Jersey Mountains, and right up against the sometimes violent river.

When my sister and I started to school, we attended the small school in Bushkill on the Pennsylvania side, but as soon as the river froze over to a safe depth, we walked across the Delaware to the larger and nearer school in Flatbrookville. Our father and our neighbor received permission to do this, temporarily only, until a ferry was started. However, our father had no intention of allowing the construction of a ferry at "Krupp's Place," much less a bridge. In fact, he was so averse to a crossing of any kind that he didn't even tell travelers about Dingman's Ferry just a few miles to the north of us. You see, he had seven or more boats to rent, and "Krupp's Place" had numerous bedrooms to let.

Leaving the waterfront for a bit, I will give you just a little more description of this Edenic spot that was my home for about six years. Behind our house was a narrow lane for any traffic, but mostly campers and vacationers from Philadelphia, who came with a boat and often spent weeks on both shores of our river. Back at the lane, and very abruptly, rose what we called a small mountain, but actually it was a bit of a hill that sloped lazily to the waterfront. I'll never forget the huckleberries and wild strawberries that we picked by the dishpanful. We called it Strawberry Hill.

The lane back of the house created the dead end to the river after winding down through a part of Pike County and down the slope we called Chestnut Hill. Here is where the fun started, for just as soon as our father decided the ice was thick enough he let us take our sleds down. After our mother's thorough bundling, we started for the top of Chestnut Hill where the long, slow ride began, for it was not really steep. When we arrived at the river's edge, we continued right on for a long way out on the river's ice. I'm sure now that our father made a track ahead of time, for it seemed like a very smooth ride. On Sunday he would get the sleigh down from the summer quarters in the "wash house," hitch a horse to it, and what a ride we had! Mother said it was our time to be elegant, for we were riding in what had been a "surrey with a fringe." I remember seeing that black thing hanging awkwardly in the supply house.

It seems to me it was a continuing good time we had, but the best was at Christmastime. There were not many presents, but I remember Elizabeth got a large, many-jointed doll with a very fancy dress, curls, and even shoes that laced up.

My doll was not as big, and probably not as expensive, but I was not as big as Elizabeth. I don't know what William unwrapped, or if our parents exchanged gifts, but it was a wonderful time we had, with oranges, more candy than was usually bought for us, also fancy cookies and nuts. Mother always had something baked for any occasion, whether we had company or not. I remember the next Christmas our beautiful dolls had new outfits. We took very good care of our toys, as we couldn't afford new things every year.

I remember our mother had a beautiful Swiss pocket watch, as she called it. She did pin it onto the upper part of her dress. She also had small diamonds in her earrings for pierced ears. They were the only jewelry I remember her wearing, in addition to a plain wedding band.

Once, when visiting my mother's cousin William in Torresdale on the Delaware, a suburb of Philadelphia, he said, "Come on and take an extra day or two. I'll take you in the cruiser right up to the spot where you lived." I wanted to go, but when I left, I promised my husband and I would be back in time to assist with a sale at the store. Instead of being thanked for my loyalty to husband and business, I was berated for foregoing the opportunity.

7

I MUST HAVE worn out my memory capabilities as a child, for I recalled things to Mother that she said a child of three could not possibly remember. Today, I lose my train of thought in seconds.

We were planning a visit to friends whom we had visited in the past. I said, "I am glad we are going to the Traugher's — they have lots of things to play with. Mother said, "You can't remember them. You were just about three years old when we were there." I told her that they had a gate we could swing on, a bird in a cage that said, "Hello, Polly wants a cracker," and there was a piece of chewing gum in the middle of a big round table that Elizabeth and I could not reach. I also recall the many flowers in vases in the house and in their garden. I guess there wasn't much Mother could say about that.

The poor horses had trouble pulling our spring wagon up that hill we referred to as "the mountain road," probably much like the roads in the hilly area here in the Ozarks years ago. As far back as I can recall, I have felt sorry for horses. If they were race horses, they were constantly prodded to make them go faster. They had to pull the plow no matter how far back the master started the point of the plow, and no matter how heavy the load, they were expected to keep it moving. I probably cried when the determined master used the whip on them. I despise cruelty, especially to horses that get nothing but a bit of food, a stall and, with a little luck, a bit of grazing.

Back then, it was difficult to visit and return the same day in daylight, even if the trip was just ten miles round trip.

We visited our friends there later when their two daughters didn't pay much attention to us any more. They were nearly teenagers and we were still kids, and a nuisance to them.

Years later, when a car balked at the foot of a hill, all the expletives in the world would be useless. I can remember the passengers stepping out, walking up the hill, and the car leisurely following behind them!

8

AS WAS NOT unusual when necessity required adjustment of a rule, I started the first grade just after my fifth birthday, along with sister Elizabeth, two years older. Bad health had held her back. Of course, we did not have the convenience of some kind of vehicle such as today's school buses. It was a matter of getting there however we could.

We were in the same grade through all of public school; in fact, we shared the double seat that was popular at that time. All grades were taught in the same room.

In the winter the river was sometimes dangerous due to the various stages of freezing, sometimes too icy to row the boat across, but not solid enough to walk on. There was a school on the west bank, but it was a greater distance from home. We had no choice but to attend it a few weeks of the winter. Of course, in mild weather our father rowed across to the Flatbrookville school in the morning and was back to pick us up in the afternoon. No wonder many children could not attend school regularly.

There was a pretty little church, non-denominational, I suppose, beside our New Jersey school. We attended Sunday School there, and our family were regular attendants at church. Christmas programs were such fun. There would be a ceiling-high tree, well decorated and lighted, I remember, but don't remember the kind of lighting available at that time. In our home our father used candles with some kind of reflector back of each candle. We saw the beautiful tree just a few minutes, then candles were extinguished, and gifts were opened.

At the church Christmas party, there would be mesh sacks of candy, oranges and a gift for each child. Oranges and other perishables were not readily available in the winter as they are today, so were a real treat for Christmas.

The church faced a little brook or rivulet at the playground edge. The small, arched wooden bridge was a delight at recess. There were not many of us, so we could all be there uncrowded. We could throw small stones to see whose made the biggest splash or went the farthest. Big bowl-shaped leaves were fun, too, trying to see how long they stayed in sight. Some of the older boys would throw corked bottles that would stay afloat. Some would place their names inside on pieces of paper, and I think some strange creatures made the trip, too — but were dead and harmless by the end of their journey.

What a beautiful place for our first school days!

 9 

I CAN THINK back in time, to the early 1900s, about conservative measures we used which were proper and cheap, like taking up dress hems, to shorten for the next wearer; I was that one. Our shoes were soled by a professional shoe repair man. Some people sent to Sears or Wards for ready-made soles and shaped them for the new owner who nailed them on. Mother still wore corsets with stays; I don't know how they were maintained when the stays bent out of shape.

Our petticoats, worn only to Sunday School, had to be starched! We always wore hats on Easter Sunday. They were handed down also. The four corner pieces of sheets were used for pillow cases or quilts. Everything must have been discarded eventually, but I don't recall a trash bag or sack, certainly no trash collector.

Pencils were sharpened with knives as long as I can remember. Very few things were bought in metal containers like our canned vegetables and fruits today. Almost everyone used and maintained jars. Sacks were used for rice and dry beans, like navy, lima and kidney beans; also flour, sugar, salt and barley for soup and stew. Those sacks became very useful — I don't recall for what — perhaps for patching overalls that men wore, as there were some strange-looking patches to be seen!

Frugality was important in all households — you just did not buy things in such quantities as today. For instance, Mother would buy just a few yards of material for a housedress — she had very few bolts of fabric to choose from; same shortage of material for my sister's and my dresses. Mother even made our underwear with elastic through the casing at the top, and sometimes a bit of lace or a ruffle.

It is so different today, but we could do it all again if survival demanded it. I remember a lady saying, "I never had a new piece of clothing in my life. My sisters were older; I just waited my turn." She smiled as if she was proud of it.

When I lived in Pennsylvania, Flatbrookville, New Jersey was the closest town to us; it could be seen across the river. On the Pennsylvania side, Bushkill was farther from our home. There were neighbors who would call friends in Flatbrookville and tell them the news of the day.

We did not have a telephone that I recall. If we had one, our parents would not have allowed us to touch it. It was in its infancy for sure, and if it worked at all, it would have been in an uncertain manner.

The first telephone I remember was a big, box-like piece, taller than wide, with a heavy thing hung on the side from a cord. That is what we called the "receiver." It was held close to the ear, and with luck you could understand what someone on the other end was saying. That person talked into the mouthpiece that stuck out from the box on his wall. Naturally I can't describe how it worked, even though the same principle works today — just modernized and improved with every passing year.

I don't know when the telephone directory first came out. We all knew the numbers from memory, and not everyone had a telephone. The people on the farms seemed to be more eager for them as they did not feel so isolated.

I remember the "party line." When a call was made, the bell on the phone would ring in five or six homes. You recognized your call by the number of rings they made in the general office — we called it the "switchboard." I'll never forget how exciting it was to hear the phone ring a short ring, another short ring, and a long one. That was our number on the "party line."

Even though some folks knew the ring was not theirs, they would take down the receiver anyway and listen to their neighbor's conversation. That was a problem in several ways. Apparently the power decreased with too many receivers down from the hook.

Party lines were a help in the country. If they had seen their neighbor down the road driving away from his home, you could answer the ring with this: "They are not at home. I just saw them drive by our house."

My daughter had a friend who was on a party line, who liked to keep in touch with the neighbors. Now and then she would listen in on another's conversation. In this case she removed the receiver, but did not say a word. The person being called answered and said, "I know you're on there, Velma. I can hear the turkeys gobbling." (Velma had a turkey farm a few miles down the road.)

10

IN FLATBROOKVILLE, PROBABLY the most impressive business was the saloon, as we called them then. I don't think it was a disreputable place that the townfolk frowned upon. It just had more lights and a pretty stained glass in the front door. Most of their customers were men.

My father had some insurance papers that had the name of "Krohn" on them, so maybe Mr. Krohn also dealt in that business.

Mrs. Krohn seemed like a very pleasant lady; she was always dressed up in what we would call "Sunday best," so perhaps she was the waitress if they served food. She was often around the place when people walked by, and she spoke to everyone and smiled. She jokingly said to my mother, "Mrs. Klee, you have four children and I don't have any. You should let them visit me once in a while. Joanna there, wouldn't you like to come and stay overnight sometime?" Another time, she approached my mother again. Knowing my mother, I would say that she used some pretty harsh words, for she was quick-tempered at times.

I really think I would have cried if Mother had let Mrs. Krohn have me overnight; I was reluctant to sleep in anyone else's bed, because I was a "bed-wetter." Not every night, but quite often. The sheets hanging on the clothesline other than our regular wash day told me I had done it again. Either the doctor or someone else told my mother that there was nothing wrong with me — I was just a sound sleeper.

11

I KNOW WE all loved our home in Pennsylvania which we called Strawberry Hill. Well-named for the wild strawberries that grew here, and we could play there as freely as the strawberries grew year after year.

Our house was large; there was a big kitchen. Next to it was what was called the sitting room, where one entertained guests or tended some "business," and where we had "no business" going. We had to trespass at night when going to bed, as the curving little stairs started in the sitting room. Then there was the parlor, just for guests or visitors. In it started another stairway they used to get to guest bedrooms, of which there were several. There was a very long porch on the front part of the house.

A few yards past the corner of the porch was the beginning of the "wash-out," as we called it. It was made many years before by flood waters when the river overflowed its banks. Another house had apparently traveled along in the water and caught onto something, then gradually broke apart, releasing some of its contents that could not float. Our father found several things in the ground when he plowed in the low places. He pulled out the headboard of a bed, a part of a stove, a man's jewelry box with a few tie pins still in it, and several other pieces. My mother said, "John, you had better stop digging, or the end of the house will fall off."

We loved our kitchen the most of all those rooms. It was not just for cooking, but was also the dining room, sitting room and parlor, in the wintertime. Each room had a separate heating unit and would require much tending and wood-carrying if we used them all. I remember an opening in the kitchen ceiling, right over our big stove. There was a grate over the hole for safety. That kept our two bedrooms over the kitchen warm enough so we all slept there. The other bedrooms were used only for our company and occasionally for paying guests who could not cross the river to the village of Flatbrookville before dark, or for fear of ice on it. In those days, people tried to keep a spare bed ready for an "overnighter."

I have described the inside of our home in Pennsylvania. Now I want to give a little description of the yard and meadow surrounding our home we called Strawberry Hill.

Behind our house was a narrow lane for traffic, mostly campers and vacationers from Philadelphia who spent time on both shores of the river. The lane ended at the foot of a promontory which was too steep to continue a road. To the west was Chestnut Hill. What a spot for a home — Chestnut Hill on the west, meadow on the south, Strawberry Hill on the north and the river on the east!

A short path led us from our big house to a ridge of sand left by flood waters many years before. It was my sister's and my playground. We stuck empty bottles into the sand, then found pretty wild flowers and stuck them into the bottle necks. There were our ladies shopping in the "hat store."

One more memory comes to mind about Strawberry Hill. The meadow close to our house had been a testing ground for a new variety of apples and other fruit. The apples were large and juicy, but fell before they were ready to be used; they broke when they hit the ground. It must have impressed me greatly, for I remember Mother saying, "Those apples are as big as Louise's head." Louise was our precious little sister who did not live longer than her fifth month.

12

NO DOUBT, MANY of my readers are aware of the beauty of Pennsylvania and the Delaware River that separates it from the New Jersey shores. I was too young when we moved there to fully enjoy the beauty of the area. I just remember the "fun" things, like riding in the boats with my father, even at night when he left the house to check his own fishing lines or to assist in some way the campers who spent weekends on our side of the river. If his first little boy had lived, he would have been a better companion, but I remember my father acting very proud of me and making sure that I was safe, admonishing me to sit still in the boat, etc.

A dentist from Philadelphia made regular weekend trips to Krupp's Place, as our resort was called. He sometimes brought his little daughter with him. Her names was "James," pronounced the same way as if it were for a boy. I recall a dress James wore that had a sailor collar, white with blue stripes and red stars in the corner. I was a bit younger, but I was always glad when she came with her father. We rode in his boat that had a motor in it, and he did not use the oars until he got to the shore.

Sometimes a man would stay in one of our guest rooms upstairs, but I don't remember seeing any of them. Now and then, one would have breakfast with our parents, but it was too early for us to go downstairs and be a nuisance.

The most unusual "overnighter" we had was a man who thought he could make it across the river by jumping from one block of ice to another as it was breaking up. He didn't fall in, but slipped far enough to get his feet and trousers soaked. I don't know how he managed for dry socks, but perhaps my father had an extra pair. I'm sure Father didn't have a drawer full of extras as he would have today.

13

OUR WASH HOUSE served many other of our needs besides housing the laundry equipment.

It was where we hung smoked meat from the rafters and also the parts of our carriage that we did not need the year round, like the sled runners when there was no snow. You have heard of the "carriage with the fringe on top." That is what it was — I don't remember using it often. What I do recall is heating bricks, wrapping them somehow, and taking them in a "spring wagon," or later in a car, to keep our feet warm. I was only four or five years old, so didn't worry about all the trouble our parents had, trying to keep us healthy, happy and warm.

I have mentioned the wash house, and there was the store house and the chicken house, but I must not forget another adjunct that all our homes had in town or on farms. That is the outhouse, also known as the privy, all of which preceded the indoor bathroom.

This little house, which had two round holes with or without lids, was the recipient of several things, including harsh treatment on Halloween night, especially in remote areas. Groups of teenage boys would go through dark backyards and upset the outhouses. It may have been considered a prank by the boys who had eight or ten in their group to upset the building, but it was a chore for the men of the homes to run down enough neighbors to restore the little building to its proper position. Not only would they turn over the little building, but even carry it away to a neighbor's yard — not a big chore for a group of big boys.

The outhouse was also the store house for all those big heavy catalogs from the mail order stores that were sent out every year or so.

The big beautiful bathrooms, with those extras like the hot tub, jacuzzi, etc. that are built today, have spoiled the fun for some, but what a welcome change — but no destruction, and no trips outside on a cold night.

Halloween night is now celebrated in a delightful way, especially for the little folks who love to dress up in funny and cute clothes, with lots of makeup. They don't need all that candy that they get in response to knocks at the door, but we all enjoy them every year. We keep the lights on the porch lit so we don't miss any of our little callers.

14

WE HAVE ALL heard the phrase, "My mother cooked this or that," and exclaim over this delicacy. Mother's food preparation varied considerably from today's methods, of course, due to fewer timesavers such as food processors and mixers, etc. We did use a hand-operated food grinder, the cheese grater and the rolling pins. The rolling pin was a "must" for making noodles. The dough was rolled into paper-thin sheets, then hung over the back of the kitchen chair to dry. When almost dry, it was rolled into a broomstick-size roll and cut into wide, medium or thin noodles, depending on the dish being prepared. They were delicious.

Making cottage cheese at home was a messy sort of job, for the strained curds of milk needed to be separated from the water, the "whey," by being put into a hanging sack to drip for hours. It was worth the trouble.

Mother's dumplings almost became famous — in the neighborhood at least. They would be light as a feather and varied in size from a large marble to a tennis ball. Some would have chopped parsley or other seasoning — some just rested on top of the stew or floated in the gravy. There were also tiny dumplings scraped very fast from the bowl of dough with a large knife, into the rapidly boiling water, so they would not stick together. They were a great favorite. I never learned to make them like Mother's.

We sometimes had kohlrabis as a vegetable. It's also called "turnip cabbage," since it looks like a turnip with the leaves growing around it instead of on the top. Mother liked it. We children didn't! But we had to try it at least. We could never flatly refuse to try any food.

I can truly say that I would sacrifice a beloved treasure if I could make my mother's sliced apple cake which we had for breakfast almost every Sunday morning. It was made with a rich dough pressed into a 9 x 12 pan rather carelessly, with a few lumps here and there. Fresh apples were peeled and thinly sliced and arranged on the top in rows. The mixture of cinnamon, sugar and something liquid was poured over the top, then baked, and we ate it warm. It was "food for the gods."

We usually had cooked cereal for breakfast, like farina, which is cereal cooked with other things to flavor. It was also used in puddings. We did not drink coffee until we were adults. We always had tea. Mother made most of our bread. Oh, that first slice right out of the oven, with real butter!

We never had hard-crusted fried chicken that is so popular today. Our chicken would be baked or used with other things like noodles or rice.

Mother was the only person I ever saw who peeled potatoes so thinly that they were nearly transparent — but eyes were dug out. She was also unique in that she scraped the carrots instead of peeling them, to benefit from the most nutritious part.

Our pies were more like cobblers — no lower crust. "You don't need all that lard," she would say. Substitutes for lard came shortly after, I'm sure, for I remember different containers she used.

The combination of prunes and dried apricots cooked together made a popular, healthy dessert.

I should have learned cooking from her — not by myself.

15

MOTHER LIKED SOFT water for washing our hair. I believe everyone had well water, even though some of us had a sink in the kitchen and a pump at one side of it.

We tried to harness rain water for our hair. It was hard work trying to save some that had not washed off a big roof on its way down to the barrel that stood below the gutter and the downspout. Some houses did not have gutters, so they kept a few large wide-mouthed cans or barrels with lids to avoid any kind of unwanted material from falling into them. Without disturbance, everything settled to the bottom, so we always had nice water for our hair. What a chore to go out and get a bucket full compared with today!

We all had lots of hair, so our method for shampooing must have been a good one.

Today's conditions supply what our faucet water lacks, and it is certainly preferred over trying to keep the lid on the barrel and all foreign matter out, like bugs, leaves and hands trying to float a boat or retrieve a ball, etc.

Young people will never appreciate the conveniences we have today, like turning on the faucet with barely a touch. If hot water is needed, the bit of waiting required is a nuisance!

If we need a light? The flip of the switch on the wall takes only a few seconds. Way back in time we did not leave a small light on all night. We had to fumble around in the night or early morning for a match to light the lamp.

If we want a bit more heat when we rise in the morning? A jump to the gadget on the wall and a hop back into bed for a few minutes takes care of everything.

If you put a cup of water with a spoon full of Sanka into the microwave for a minute and a half, you will have a cup of hot coffee waiting for you after you rush out to pick up the morning paper.

Your great-grandfathers would be trying to get the heating stove going, and great-grandma would be coaxing the kitchen stove to hurry with boiling the coffee — no percolators yet. She would probably rush to the cellar for a bit of ham or bacon to go with the eggs for breakfast. There were so many morning chores, one wonders how all the work was done, especially on the farm where animals of all kinds were needing care, too.

16

HAD IT NOT been the home where we lost a five-month-old baby girl and two stillborn baby brothers, I believe we would have been very happy to stay at Strawberry Hill indefinitely. It was a vacation area where my father operated and supplied various camps frequented by people from the cities. Swimming, boating, fishing, etc. were enjoyed by the well-to-do. Motors on boats had appeared, and even a canvas tent fastened to the side of the automobile was seen now and then. It was quite a curiosity on 1910, no doubt. Our little church in Flatbrookville, across the river, would welcome all comers, I'm sure, disregarding all denominational differences.

But fate stepped in and changed our plans and our lives. In the early part of 1910, Mother's Uncle Gustav Knauer had moved his family to Wilson, Kansas, a small town about 60 miles west of Salina. His trade was carpentry. I do not remember anything about the family being discussed heretofore, only that he was in dire straits due to his wife's death, leaving him with six young children. For some reason not known to me, he contacted our family for assistance — not financial but helpful advice from a caring relative. He begged us to visit him and perhaps suggest a solution for one in his predicament.

It was in the middle of winter, and hardly the time of year one would choose to take four children aged from three to nine halfway across the United States. Train engines were using coal then. I don't know how passenger cars were heated or if they had sleeping compartments yet. Everything was less comfortable than today. We changed trains in St. Louis. Mother did not like anything in the West so far.

I do recall my three-year-old brother William looking out the coach window and exclaiming in a rather loud voice, "Look at all those cows. They are all mine." Everybody laughed; he was a very cute, blond, curly-haired little boy whom people exclaimed about.

We arrived in Wilson in the dark of the night and were met by Uncle Gus as they called him. It was only about three blocks, maybe four, from Union Pacific Depot to our uncle's house. I don't know if he had horses — I don't think he had an auto yet. Everyone carried something. People did not think of every inconvenience being a hardship as they do today.

The road was unpaved, as were most side roads and streets. If there was a street lamp, I don't remember it — I just know it was very dark! There were electric lights in some homes, but the coal oil lamp was still the most popular for lighting the home. Children don't remember the important things, but I have a photo of Uncle Gus' family stretched out across the front of the house (to be sure everyone would be seen). It was a nice two-story white frame house with lots of shrubbery, and the lamps were all lit up for us.

17

THIS CHAPTER IS simply a description of the little town of Wilson, Kansas, which would be our home for the next nine years. I believe its population was about 1,200 until Interstate 70 was put in, and Wilson suffered thereby. Instead of dropping down from a straight line to pick up Wilson, they put in a secondary route off the highway to serve it. I believe the population dropped considerably as a result.

To know why Wilson was such a good place to live at that time is to see here just what it consisted of. Here are just some of the businesses and buildings the downtown had:

- Central Hotel
- Midland Hotel
- Farmer's State Bank
- Wilson State Bank
- Schermerhorn's Department Store
- Daylight Department Store
- Swedish Church
- Presbyterian Church
- Methodist Church
- Catholic Church near brick schoolhouse
- Large grain elevator
- Two grocers
- Two-story brick schoolhouse
- Park with a bandstand
- Nice Union Pacific depot
- Jewelry and music store
- Lumber yard

- Shoe repair shop
- Opera house/theater
- Wilson World newspaper
- Pool hall
- Smith's Restaurant
- Offices of various kinds
- Blacksmith shop
- Barber shop

I don't recall ever seeing a beauty parlor. Ladies all had long hair, the longer the better, the bigger the knot or roll. Can you imagine a town of this size today having all these stores, etc., and still having good old Montgomery Ward to order from?

18

IN WILSON, WE rented a small house, all that was available at the time. Mother started immediately to prepare it for occupancy, but with forced enthusiasm, no doubt, for she loved the eastern U.S.A. and its proximity to sisters and brothers who had settled there.

Since Uncle Gus had quite a family of his own, we needed to move our family of six somewhere, even for a short stay. For a brief time, there was discussion about Uncle Gus' dilemma. I remember being at his home often, but do not remember what solution was made. The cousins were all older than sister Elizabeth and me.

One day our father was getting ready to take the train to Strawberry Hill. We were told he would be back soon. He had gone to prepare for the permanent move to Wilson. What an expense that move by train must have been! Today there would be an estate or moving sale. Perhaps there was a partial one at least. I feel sure there were no vehicles big enough to move a house full of furniture.

When our father returned with our furniture and other possessions from Strawberry Hill, he spent some time looking at land, visiting Smokey Hill River, and mixing with town folk, etc. Euphoria soon changed to disappointment. He realized that his experience as resort operator was useless around Wilson and the general area. (In recent years, a big dam has been built, and it may have some kind of place now for a man with his expertise.) Our father was a dedicated outdoor man, not tall, but rugged as I remember him. Apparently, foresightedness was not one of his characteristics. Around Wilson, one could easily appreciate that you were a farmer or had a business sufficient in itself — no outside help needed.

When our father was offered the job of handling a crew of men who were going into Canada to a big lumbering project, he was instantly interested. Except for considerable book work, he would be outside. Of course, the family would follow soon. Mother said, "Only if there is a good school." Sister Elizabeth and I hoped for a place where the mothers used several languages as our mother did. Her difference embarrassed us in Wilson. Little did we realize that our mother's linguistic aptitude was admirable and set her apart commendably.

We children did not take notice of preparations being made for our father's departure. It was just like we did when preparing for a weekend visit with a relative back east. I suppose it was just as well that none of us knew we would never see Father again. I was only a child of six or seven, just old enough to remember him playing with us, making things with cockle burrs, which grew in profusion around there, and laughing at what he had made.

I also recall going to the depot and seeing him step up into the coach, trying to laugh and wave.

19

I SHOULD MENTION some small but lingering incidents that happened in the first place we lived in Wilson. Since they have stayed with me through all these years of major events, they must have some merit in my story.

Our first house was next to the Lyndels. May Lyndel was in our class. We had not met her family at this time.

I noticed a nice long rope swing in their back yard. No one was around, so I took a ride, and it was just the right "accompaniment" for my song. I always liked to sing from as far back as memory takes me. It was fun — the higher I could swing, the louder I would sing. A lady appeared at the back door and said, "Little girl, do not sing so loud; we have a very sick man in the house and he is trying to sleep. You better go home." I was really offended, and even more so when Mother said, "You don't go into other people's yards." Where we lived at the little resort, we could go almost any place.

That was my first offense and rejection. We soon moved to a bigger house with better bathing facilities and an electric light hanging from the ceiling! Everything was better — a bigger yard, a little rippling stream beside us, and our back door faced the back door of the family across the alley. Those were the days when most homes had alleys for convenience.

The family at the back also had three children near our ages: Rosie, Blanch and John Helm. Their father had a big lumber yard. We soon played with Rosie and John and went in and out of each other's back doors. Just inside their door there was a pin cushion on a window sill and the prettiest little pin on it that I had ever seen — it was two hearts, one overlapping the other, and probably "gold" from Woolworth's or Kresge's. No one ever wore it — it was always there. So I took it and pinned it on my dress. No one seemed to notice it, but the next day Mrs. Helm sent Rosie to our house. She wanted to borrow our egg beater and wanted Joanna to bring it over. Instantly I knew she had seen that pin on my dress, and I was scared and crying. I think I knew that what I did was stealing. I ran right over there, threw the pin into the back door and ran. I think my mother and Mrs. Helm had it all planned, for I was never scolded. Who knows, maybe a professional thief was "nipped in the bud."

Across the little rippling stream I mentioned was a family by the name of Williams; they had a boy named Hal. He seemed grown up, but was about 12 or 13. I was in our back yard, singing again, bothering no one. All of a sudden he stopped throwing stones into the water and was throwing them at me. I suppose I said something he resented, for the next thing I realized was that I was lying on the ground and my head hurt. There was also a bleeding bump that Mother had to tend to. My experience with the rope swing proved I was no prima donna, but I never should have been "stoned," as a common criminal would have been in the Dark Ages, for a bad song.

20

IN WILSON WE were always moving, it seems, trying to find something just right for our family. The third house we occupied was on the northwest fringe of the city limits, if they had city limits then. It was considerably farther from our school which was in the southeast part of town. Everyone walked to school in Wilson, whether hot or cold, sunny or stormy. As I said before, your two feet were your only conveyance. The jeweler — music store owner, Mr. Slimm, and one of the McKittricks had a little car, but they were not seen on the streets often, maybe just for a Sunday afternoon ride.

So I had to walk to Mrs. Hoopes' house. She was a lonely little lady that Mother heard about. Mother's habit was fixing little special things to eat and sharing them with people who seemed to be in need of treats that they could not prepare for themselves.

Mrs. Hoopes was very old; her house smelled very old, too, because the doors were always closed and locked. I had gone with Mother several times and remember the house well — every room but the kitchen had the shades pulled.

One thing Mrs. Hoopes liked best was vegetable soup — very healthy, with beef broth and barley. When we had that for our family, Mother would partially fill a little metal bucket that had a tight lid and a bail for carrying it. It was my job to carry it the short distance to Mrs. Hoopes' house. About halfway there, a little black and white dog would run out at me, to play perhaps, but I was always afraid of dogs I did not know about. I would start to run, and the dog would follow and bark and nip at my heels. One days he caught his tooth on my long stocking and tore a hole in it. Mother was really unhappy about that. She said, "He runs after you to keep up with you. Stop and he will stop. He just wants to play." I don't remember if his tail was wagging, but Mother was probably right. I still made the soup and food deliveries, but was always afraid.

I think Mrs. Hoopes was a very sad old lady with no family any place. One day when Mother visited her, she asked if I could stay overnight sometime. I don't remember if I was pleased or unwilling, but I had to sleep with Mrs. Hoopes in that room that had an old smell that you get in attics.

That poor little lady did not live very long after that — someone found her in her bed. I guess I granted her wish one time anyway.

21

WE TAKE OUR conveniences for granted these days. Even those of us who do not have the luxuries the rich enjoy can somehow afford enough heat and light, food, etc., sufficient for our simple living.

Listed below are some of the differences in the teens, and probably earlier, that existed when I was growing up.

In the grocery stores, you could buy a long string of wieners (hot dogs) for 15 cents, chewing gum 1 cent a stick, and that is the quantity many of us bought. The butcher would cut as small a piece of meat as was wanted (probably to enhance vegetable soup). Our candy was button-sized red hots — a half-dozen for a penny; white Martha Washington squares, about 1-1/4" for 1 cent each. Pickles were in open barrels in some places. Flour and sugar were bought in big sacks, which were later used for quilts and other sewing projects. Many people had a few chickens that ate scraps, etc., potato peelings and just about anything. I don't remember hamburger, in stores or on buns.

There were no icemen delivering to homes, as was popular in the '30s. Mother kept a container she could lower into the well — it held our butter, milk, meat, etc. She wrapped rapidly deteriorating fruit like pears in newspaper and buried them just beneath the surface of the ground.

About our school clothes: we wore our dresses five days a week. After Monday, Tuesday and Wednesday, we wore a pinafore tied in back, to cover any soil on the dress. It may have been the pinafore first, then removed for the rest of the week,

I'm not sure. Remember, any washers at that time were hand-operated, and some families were still heating the iron on the kitchen stove. And we ironed almost everything. Sheets were partly folded before ironing, and many pieces got the "once-over," like pillow cases, towels, tablecloths, napkins (no paper ones yet). The clothing pieces had to be carefully done — no wrinkles. Elizabeth and I helped a great deal with ironing.

I want to mention here — in cold weather in Kansas, we wore long knit underwear — our stockings were pulled up over that. We all walked to and from school, so warm clothes were a necessity in winter.

What was called the "bathroom" was given a misnomer in most homes. We had a stool and wash basin, but we still took the bath in a wash tub in the kitchen, with the shades pulled, and hurried before the water cooled. The next bather was waiting — the water needed to be carried out and fresh put in, half cold and half from water well in the stove. In some families, I understand, the water was not changed, so you hoped to be first in line!

We had a mending day — usually middle of the week, after washing and ironing. Mother taught us the art of darning, the most disliked job being that of picking up all the stitches around the hole, then weaving up and down and across, thereby making it wearable. She was an expert at this job.

We had a nice Singer treadle sewing machine for as long as I can remember. It is probably still operable but resting in an antique shop somewhere.

I don't want to overlook our postage prices — the 2-cent stamp for letters and 1-cent post card. Hard to believe — 37 cents for a stamp, and I've been told another raise is imminent.

22

THEN THERE WAS the weekly wash day — Monday. Mother was completely in charge of that. The washer was hand-operated. Two tubs were used for rinsing — we called it "first and second rinse," to be sure all the soap was gone. There were a few boxed soap flakes around — I just remember "Aunt Jemima's." Many of us saved bacon grease or any other grease to be used in making home-made soap. If done properly, it was as white as snow. During the First World War years, it was one of the commodities that was often scarce. (I made it numerous times during the Second World War.) The only trouble was, you had to "flake" it yourself with a knife. The next step was hanging the clothes on a clothesline outside, getting that bit of natural fresh air into them. When dry, some of the clothes were slightly dampened and rolled loosely before ironing, to get the wrinkles out.

Tuesday was ironing day — all three of us worked at that. It was a chore before electricity. The irons were very heavy — the flat part was heated on top of the stove. By having two or more irons heating, you could alternate them and always have a hot one ready. Did we ever scorch anything? We sure did. To avoid that, you would clamp on the handle, stick one finger in your mouth to moisten it, then quickly touch the iron with it. The degree of sizzle you got would tell you when it was just right.

Electric irons were a blessing and time-saving. There was no permanent press material until much, much later. It has been one of our greatest inventions, but nothing feels as comfortable as cotton. Many people defer to comfort in these more carefree times; a few wrinkles here and there don't matter. Had we had the stretchy "knits" 30 years sooner, we who ironed everything would have better backs today.

 23 

IT SEEMS THAT more thought was given to the style of dress than to its maintenance. Ladies' very best "Sunday-go-to-meetin'-dress" would be taffeta, velvet or some other material that would not allow laundering. I don't recall any kind of dry-cleaning. Men's suits were never washable; of course, they were only worn for special occasions, like weddings and funerals. I have heard numerous times that a man was buried in the same suit he was married in.

At home I think all our clothes were washable. Probably our coats were never cleaned — just well cared for — brushed, and always hung up. I remember coats being "put away" for winter. Moth balls had a hand in that treatment. I remember hanging them outside to air out.

I wonder what the ladies did about the fancy tucks, pleats, lace and huge watermelon-shaped sleeves that were worn by the rich ladies who danced the waltzes and attended the operas.

24

I HAVE BEEN asked a few times, "Did you go to the doctor for check-ups, etc.?" No, not for check-ups — only when we were really sick. Even then, we did not go to the doctor — he came to us. Mother knew how to treat ordinary illnesses like colds or a bit of stomach ache. My brother, John, who was premature and never really well, was taken to the doctor's office regularly, like once a month.

A cold treatment that is out of date today was applying goose grease to the neck and rubbing it in well. Even the chest got that treatment for a bad cough. I don't recall it being used on me, but it must have been at some time, as I know the odor from it was terrible. Another treatment that cost nothing was tying the heavy sock you wore that day around your neck and leaving it on all night. As far back as I can recall, we used Vicks salve, applied by Mother. My father's treatment was a teaspoon of whiskey and a bit of water, poured into a saucer. Then he lit a match to the mixture to burn off the alcohol. Then it was ready for the patient to swallow, then hop into bed with lots of covers. No, Father was not a drinker, for I remember that same old bottle in the cabinet — the only one that was ever there.

About skin care — we just used soap and water and splashed with cold water to close the pores. Ivory soap was in our house for baths, and usually home-made soap for laundry. I remember long pans of white soap that Mother made and cut into bars. Any kind of grease was used — just well strained. Later on we used the flakes — no more shaving the bar soap.

My first face cream was Pond's. I think there was just one kind. Today there is a variety — dry skin, regular, etc. We did not have shelves of shampoo to choose from, and certainly not liquids. Vaseline took care of lots of things and is still popular for rough hands, etc.

 # 25 

PERHAPS SOMETHING SIMILAR to this has happened elsewhere and not just in Wilson, where we spent most of our school years.

The main line of the Union Pacific Railroad ran right through Wilson, and I believe it stopped frequently. It certainly delivered a lot of packages for Sears, Roebuck & Company, Montgomery Wards and other businesses. We had a bigger town of Hays to the west, and Manhattan and Salina a greater mileage to the east, where we could go by train, which Wilsonians did occasionally, but some things were bought in small amounts right from our local merchants.

How this happened I never knew, but it was a pleasant surprise. A carload of apples became stranded on the railroad's siding. It was announced to the teacher in our school that upon dismissal all children could go to the apple car and get as many apples as they could eat. The railroad folks did not want to be left with a carload of rotten apples, I guess.

The teachers in each room chose one of her pupils to go to the front of the room and make the announcement for his or her room. My sister Elizabeth was chosen for our room. Although I was just a looker and listener, I was as proud as if I had been chosen. Clapping, instigated by the teacher, of course, followed the announcement.

I suppose we all had apples or applesauce for dessert that night. Elizabeth and I were cited for being the only ones who said "thank you." My mother's stern adherence to courtesy paid off in that instance.

As my readers know by now, I am a very old lady. Ninety-eight is old! I grew up when manners were the first thing we learned. Saying "please" and "thank you" were among the first rules that were enforced, and I'll admit I never forgot them. A young mother I knew disagreed with me. She said, "Children shouldn't need to be thanking all the time." I agree, they don't need to make a big thing of it — just a simple "thanks" or "please" makes an impression, and they enjoy doing it, and all their lives they will do it naturally.

26

I HAVE BEEN asked numerous times, "What did you do for entertainment?" There was no radio, television and few cars.

We did more for entertainment than people do today. On five weekdays we went to school, of course, walking to and from, with as near perfect record as possible. Before we moved to a different location, we walked home for lunch. I believe we took sandwiches sometimes, and an apple was usually the dessert. In cities there would be some kind of transportation or a cafeteria. In Wilson, there were just your two feet.

Occasionally, there would be a "motion picture" at the opera house, as we called it, because now and then there would be a "stage play," just foolish acts, accompanied by some kind of music (fiddler, etc.). We did not attend them often. I remember a "still" picture accompanied by the conversation printed below it. You had to read fast and have good eyesight. Here are weekend activities we enjoyed: We took talks, read a great deal, took part in church activities and visited friends. We had an Edison phonograph with an amplifier that looked a lot like a morning glory on a stand. The neighbors loved it; they wanted to hear Galli Circi, the famous Italian coloratura soprano; John McCormick, famous Irish tenor, and Jenny Lind, Swedish colorature soprano of the late 1880s. We had numerous records, shaped like Campbell soup cans, with top and bottom cut out. Today you would call the reception we got "very poor," for they were squeaky sometimes, and disappointing when the machine ran out of "juice" in the middle of the record. All you needed to do was raise the needle from the record and crank it up again.

Mother taught us to knit; someone taught us to crochet, tat and make a long cord through an empty spool with a crochet hook. You needed to put four little tacks on top of the spool.

We sewed on Sunday on our treadle Singer machine. Some people said, "No sewing on Sunday!" We took snapshots in the park with a box camera. Mother let us iron on Saturday or Sunday — just clothes we wore to school. We darned and mended stockings — there were no nylon hose in general use; they were just coming in and were a nuisance, trying to keep the seams straight. Yes, they really had seams up the back!

We made valentines in season and wrote letters. Later, we had a piano — we all loved to sing and try to play. Children would roller skate, hopscotch, play ball, make paper or doll clothes, do crafts with crayons, etc. We played games outside and card games such as "Old Maid" and "Flinch." For May Day, we made our own May baskets with flowers and cookies, and the children loved delivering them to neighbors.

 27 

MOST OF US never gave a thought or thanks to our parents in the past for keeping us warm in the winter. Our mother took care of the "furnace" in our house. Like many six-room houses built before registers throughout the house became common, our house had one register, and that one allowed enough heat for the rooms we used during the day and evening. The kitchen stove provided sufficient heat for anyone in there. Bedrooms did not need much heat.

But this small "furnace" beneath the first floor had to be carefully handled. Too large a fire would have been hard to tend, as there was little space between the furnace and the walls, which were stone.

Like everyone did, I suppose, Mother let the fire die down toward evening. Then, before retiring, she would bank the remaining fire with ashes — even add a very solid log, and cover it with ashes also. This handling gave us a bit of warmth throughout the night, but not a dangerous blaze. In the morning it was stirred into action again and more logs were added. This was done every day.

We have all admired the huge residences built before electricity was invented. They had a fireplace in each bedroom. I have seen them in mansions open to the public. What a lot of wood-carrying that would involve. Today we need only touch the gadget on the wall for more or less warmth.

Then came the coal age — it was better and worse. It did not emit that wonderful wood-burning aroma and created more soot, but did not require so much attention. We still used a coal furnace in the early 1930s.

Do you remember the coal oil stove, that black thing about the size of a large tree trunk and about three feet high? It could be picked up and moved to any part of the house. It makes me shudder to think of babies learning to walk and inadvertently touching the stove. No wonder it has been said, "Some babies literally grew up in the crib."

28

SPELLING CLASSES WERE always my favorite part of grade school. I was not without mistakes, nor was I always best.

Sometimes we would choose up sides as equally as possible and have a real serious, exciting time. Occasionally our teacher, Miss Kyser, would vary the contest a little by writing two similar words on the blackboard. Sometimes only one word would be on the board, and at other times there would be a small sentence with or without a misspelled word.

I wish I could remember the exact sentence for our side, but I just remember it was about "lightning" and "thunder." She had written "lightening" instead and I put up my hand, but our time was up and she quickly erased the sentence. Several of the students agreed that the word was misspelled, but Miss Kyser ignored it. I wanted our side to win. Whether we were ahead at that time I don't know.

My downfall was calling out, "But it was spelled wrong." She sent me to my desk, took the ruler and hit my hands several times for "speaking out of turn." I cried, not because our side did not get credit, but because I was the only one who got her hands hit with the ruler.

I believe she said something to my mother about it, for my mother's questions indicated she knew something about it. Miss Kyser seemed extra nice after that; maybe I imagined that. Maybe we were supposed to think that teachers don't make mistakes!

While I am writing about school incidents, I'll just mention this one briefly. Our teacher, the other Miss Kyser (a cousin) had been coaching us for a test, insisting we really needed to study diligently as it would be a different kind of test.

On the hour of the test, she said she was so pleased to have seen us studying so well, how much good it would do further along in the class. "But for today's test, there are only two questions. They are similar, so be careful."

They were very similar, but I did know the right answers. Then I made my mistake. I glanced over the shoulder of the girl in front of me. She had the answer on her paper reversed. Her name was Inez, and she did well in school. My answers must be wrong, I thought. So I changed mine to match hers, and we both got a zero. I don't know that I learned a lesson, but I remember it after these eighty-some years.

 29 

IN 1914, THE WAR was raging in Europe. It became worse day by day, and by 1916 the United States became involved. For four years Great Britain, Russia, France, Italy and several other countries, then the United States also, finally defeated Germany. This war was called "First World War," World War I or the Great War. For 18 months, the hottest topics in our newspapers and conversation anywhere were about enlistments, drafts, successes and failures over there. Of course, our family was not involved personally, but it made Mother sad to hear and read about nephews from here and over there, possibly fighting and killing each other, unaware of it.

I learned many years later that John Shively (my future husband) was in the Navy on transport ships for the last 18 months of World War I. He was very young. I have a few snapshots of him in one of the bombed-out areas of France. He often related his disappointments when a boat-load of boys disembarked and had a great time looking for the fun places and, of course, the girls. But the Navy boys were kept on the boats, getting ready to sail for the United States to pick up another load of troops. He did finally get to disembark and did find some young ladies, as they were referred to. At the seaside, the girls were wearing one-piece black swim suits that hung to their knees and swimming hats that were much like Martha Washington's ruffled dust caps. *(See photo in the photo section.)*

But finally the war was over. I remember well the parades, bells ringing, people shouting, so glad for peace again and looking forward to the returning soldiers. "Colonel" Sackman was Wilson's oldest soldier. I don't know that he was a colonel — rather that he was proud to have been in the worst of the war and survived.

The aftermath was sad for quite a few Wilson families, as everywhere else, where their boys came home maimed or sick, or not at all. A teacher of one of our classes learned that her husband-to-be was killed after peace was declared. Word had not gotten to the front. How much better it is today when the news follows the action almost immediately.

How much better and fairer it would be to settle our differences sensibly, like human beings, in discussion and arbitration, instead of breaking and killing our boys (and girls today) and the hearts of people who had nothing to do with starting the wars. The war-torn boys are never appreciated to the fullest. Their ambitions have been interrupted, never to be the same as before they were called to duty, to partake in a fray they did not cause. They were simply in the right age bracket to be drafted. It was even worse in the early 1900s than today, for their comforts were not the concern they are today. It is so unfair to have a "draft board" in charge of selecting the men for compulsory military service — one having the right to tell another that he must take a chance of being killed. They must be healthy — the "cream of the crop."

I was so lucky — my brother William was in the reserves, so, of course, did not go overseas. I never had the sad good-bye to make as a family member left for war, perhaps for extinction.

30

AS I HAVE related, there were several unforgettable tragedies in Wilson in the nine years we lived there. In retrospect, the parting with our father would have been the worst for our family, had we known we would never see him again. I am sure he would not have boarded the train with a smile on his face and a casual wave of his hand, had he anticipated or feared the outcome of his trip.

A major, sorrowful time in Wilson was the influenza epidemic of 1919. No doubt, there were other cities and towns that suffered greater losses in number, but in a small town like Wilson where everyone knew everyone else, it seemed a greater catastrophe. One family, whose name I cannot recall, lost four children. A young pregnant Mrs. Baum also died. There were opinions by some that influenza was especially severe on pregnant women. Our rural mail carrier, Barney, who made his route by motorcycle, also succumbed to the epidemic. He was a large, sturdy-looking man, not fat, but the outdoorish type. Someone commented, "If Barney can't recover from it, none of us can."

I can recall warnings posted inside the front door, such as "MEASLES," CHICKEN POX," etc., which meant DO NOT ENTER. I don't recall a sign for influenza. There was no hospital in Wilson while we lived there. I don't remember a physician, but there may have been one. I do recall a doctor coming to Wilson one day a week, and we took our infirm brother, John, to see him. I cannot think of anything life-threatening that could have benefited by a full-time physician, but there could have been.

We lived in a house where little twin girls were burned so severely that they died. There was a coal oil lamp that had been lit, and for some reason one of the girls bumped into the lamp. As it hit the table or floor, it broke and immediately there were flames everywhere. The sister probably tried to help, causing her clothes to catch on fire also.

That the same family would suffer another tragedy some years later is difficult to rationalize, but it did happen. The father of the twin girls also had two sons. He drove a grain wagon for the grain elevator on the other side of the train track. For a reason no one can explain since there were no witnesses, the wagon was hit by the train and the driver was killed. One of the boys was in our class.

With that much bad luck so early in life, those boys must have felt "cursed" (I don't use that word often). I know someone helped them, and they had a good education and a place in the world.

Just to "sweeten" these unfortunate incidents a bit, I may say I recall that my sister was quite enamored of the older boy. He had beautiful red hair and was aware of Elizabeth looking at him more often than casually. He was also a "brain" in the class.

31

IT USED TO be commonplace to see a huckster on the streets, selling whatever and wherever he could get the highest prices. There was also the junkman who would buy or sell. I can't remember seeing my father dealing with either one — of course, Mother wouldn't either except in later years when fresh vegetables were sold from wagons or trucks.

In the half-year I stayed in the country, I was a "front seat" witness to a deal being made. The Nelsons, where I stayed, were away from home a short time, and the school teacher, my friend with whom I shared a room, was inside when this happened.

Charles, the oldest son of the Nelson family, was about 11 years old at the time. He, being the oldest, felt important when it was up to him to answer the questions of the junkman who came up the lane from the road. The driver's conversation with Charles went something like this: "Young man, are your folks around?" With a swelling chest Charles answered, "No, they aren't. They drove to my uncle's and won't be back till supper time." The junkman was probably overjoyed. "Well, then, young man, maybe you can help me. I am collecting old stuff your father would not want any more. They are just in the way."

I was getting a little concerned when Charles opened the door of the tool shed and exposed all the contents, most of which were too large for the junkman's wagon. The man said something like, "Now, here are some old boots your father doesn't wear any more." They were the hip-high kind that are used to wade in when fishing.

Charles said, “No, he doesn’t wear them.” The junkman mentioned a price, under a dollar, because I heard the money jangling as he paid Charles. I felt that being about three years older than Charles, I should say something about that quick sale. I said, “Charles, you should ask your father first. Those boots look almost new. I have seen him wear them down by the creek.” But both of the “dealers” ignored me. Charles was pleased with the real money, and the junkman was probably well satisfied with the best deal he had made that day.

I was very concerned. I just knew it was not what Mr. Nelson would have done.

I was right. I did not mention it when the Nelsons returned that evening. Charles could not keep his hands out of his pockets. When his father heard the jangle, too, and asked about it, Charles tried to think of something that sounded plausible, but fear was in his voice. His father continued the questioning, and soon the whole story was out in the open.

Mr. Nelson took Charles out to the tool shed, and when he found his boots gone he went back to the house for his razor strop, then out again. I can still hear the screams from Charles that lasted a long time. When Charles did not come back in for hours it seemed, I wondered if he was dead. Of course, he wasn’t, and after a while Mr. Nelson went out and brought Charles in — told him to go to bed. Mrs. Nelson had dinner ready. The teacher came down and we all ate — but no one mentioned Charles not being there. I felt so sorry for him.

 32 

MY FATHER'S CREW gathered in International Falls, Minnesota, just across the line of the province of Ontario, then westward into Manitoba province, etc. We were always eager for his letter from those strange-sounding places, but disappointed when he wrote in German, which was a bit easier for him. He always inquired about the children first. Soon we could write small notes and include them with Mother's letters. When we had to write Saskatchewan, even Elizabeth had trouble with that. She was always first to find the new location in the atlas. She was ahead of me in everything, but I did not allow for two years' difference in age. It just made me unhappy sometimes.

As time went on, the subject of moving surfaced less often. There were pleas from our father for more letters. Mother became less communicative about those received. Sister Elizabeth and I were too young to give our parents' relationship much thought, but we may have made some inquiries, given rise by Elizabeth's intuitive mind. Our brothers were too young to miss anyone very long. But Elizabeth said to Mother one day, "Don't you write to Father any more?" I don't recall what the answer was.

Absence does not always make the heart grow fonder, or does it, for someone else? After some months, Mother seemed to have other interests, not romantic, that we noticed — just a different attitude. She exchanged letters with her siblings in New York City, New Jersey and Pennsylvania, also with her father in Germany; I suppose also with her brother over there.

Our father's name or whereabouts were not mentioned as often as heretofore — just that the crew had moved farther west, through the province of Alberta and British Columbia.

But in 1919, Mother received word that John C. Klee was missing. There had been heavy rain and flooding in British Columbia, the last province of Canada before Vancouver Island. There had been much damage to the lumber camp, including our father's quarters off the water. Soon after, what was left of his belongings was returned to us. For years afterward, we kept in touch with those who continued the search. We had a hopeful clue now and then, but nothing conclusive.

Could it be that the disappearance was deliberate? Or was there foul play? Even suicide was considered. After all, Mother was seldom seen writing, and letters had been fewer from him.

Years later I contacted the RLDS church. They are very active in genealogy and eager to help researchers. We followed every clue. On a trip to Yukon Territory many years later, I found the name "Klee" in the little phone directory that covered a vast territory. I called the number with my heart pounding with anticipation. As before, the call produced nothing. The man spoke neither English nor German and hadn't been on the continent long; a voice beside him spoke for him. We have checked many, many cemeteries. I suppose I will never really give up. I even checked Wilson's Ellsworth County for the possible divorce of our parents, but as usual, with no results.

The following letters and correspondence were found in my mother's personal effects. I had never been aware of these letters prior to this time. I could not translate the old German myself as I have only a seven-year-old's knowledge of the language.

Not until 1997, upon professional translation of these letters, did I realize what mystery they might unravel as to my father's "disappearance." The letters seem to disprove some of our relatives' opinions that he deserted us:

Gross Sottrum (?) *January 25, 1909*
Dear Son and Daughter-in-Law,

At long last I must pick up the pen and write a few lines to you hoping that you are still in good health and happy. Thank God, we are still able to say the same about ourselves, except for myself, because I am still dealing with my old disease. I can no longer work and have to take care of the stove at all times. Yet things are alright because Margaretha (?) got married and her husband is a shoemaker, who has his workshop here. In addition, he does some farming, something he enjoys doing and plans to continue. We couldn't get on with what we were able to do, because I cannot work at all. August is doing his military service and will have to complete his two years. That's too long for us to continue with that heavy work load.

We had a good year and harvested 422 bushels of rye and 366 bushels of oats. The fruits of the summer turned out very well, too. I read still in your letter referring to Leuh ... (?). If that is so, the area there must be very much like ours here. Ferto ... (?) are not particularly well, because Johann is somewhat mentally ill and grandfather is dead. The mill does not work and is no longer utilized. Moreover, they have eight children. The oldest is in military service, and two are working for other people, others are in school. They still have enough to live, but the old people had terrible debts. Dear Johann, if you know about a good place for August, he could go over there too after his military service. He knows farming very well. Here he doesn't want to follow my orders, he is wasteful. He is stationed in Schleswig with the 10th ... regiment.

Margareta's husband hails from Sch...sal, and his name is Diederich Röger. We also have a little daughter of three months. How are your little ones? Now they are still easy to handle. I always wanted to write earlier, and I don't remember who was the last one to write, you or I. It was probably me. With that I want to come to an end.

Many kind regards from all of us,

J. Klee (my father's father)

(scribbled around the margin) I have sold the mill. After my death you will have to contact Röger. I have made my last will and testament. ... do write soon.

* * * * *

(Postcard)
To: Mrs. Pauline Klee ... Kansas, Kansas, America

Michelfeld, April 1, 1912

Dear Pauline!

Here I am sending you a picture of the house in Michelfeld you were born in. Please forgive me for not writing for such a long time, for I had misplaced your last letter, and therefore I did not have your address. When you write again, send a picture of your farmyard or the entire place. I have heard that my brother Fritz will come to Germany this year. Do you know anything about that? Best regards,

Johann (?) Wurst

Letter will follow as soon as you write.

* * * * *

November 9, 1913 (1919?)

Dear Wife and Children:

I hope you received my check. I will give you my address. Now write immediately how you are. Here in Canada it is still cold. This morning it was 40 degrees below siro and three feet of snow. Let me know whether you received the money from Pinselwenin, and let me know how much you have. I shall send you more at the end of March or on April 1st. After that I would like to do some contract work. It pays more money and is quite pleasant. Five Thalers or more per day. However, no payment is made before the job is completed. And that could take as much as about four months. So let me knowhow much you have and what you think of it.

Here I must close. Many greetings to all of you,

John Klee

* * * * *

Fort Georgs, January 24, 1914

Dear Wife and Children:

Finally, I received a letter from you, and I take it that you are all in good health, which is the case with me as well. You also received the checks from me. In my last letter I wrote about your coming here that I saw from your letter that you like it better now in Wilson, which I am glad to hear. Although I would like to see that we are all together again for good, the climate is better for me here, and I can earn more money here than at your place.

Your opinion is right, for the time being, you are better off in Wilson because of the children, for the schools are better than here, what is worth a lot. I see from your letter that the girls are learning well, which makes me happy. Do buy all the books you need. I cannot understand S. Tun. It seems to me he intends to defraud us all. Do write to M. Kron or Rosenkranz. I will send you the insurance papers, you can keep them better than I. My ... has gone down for the winter months I have 40 thalers and board. These are bad times all everywhere. I am sending you a bank draft in the amount of 70 dollars. You are writing of Christian aid. How would you like to have Irmi and Willi baptized?

Regards from me to all,

John Klee

* * * * *

The things you have sent me were received, two pairs of shoes and three ... caps and gloves, for which I thank you very much. Don't send more stuff for the time being until I let you know. I still have to pay 3 dollars.

To Elizabeth and Johanna

I see from your letter that you had a good Christmas. That makes me happy. And being popular in school is great, with that you will be able to earn good money here.

To Irmi and Willie

Irmi, how are things with you? Do you want to go to school soon? Willi, it is good that you are going to school. You must have a good memory to recite that piece by heart.

Your Father

(Scribbled on margin): The Bank of Ottawa asked whether you received the draft in the amount of 40 dollars that was sent in August. If you can remember, do reply immediately.

* * * * *

Edmonton, July 14, 1914

Dear Wife and Children,

Your check was received, and I thank you very much. Dear wife, I believe it would be best for us if I would take a homestead here with 160 acres, so long as one can get it for as little as 10 dollars. That would be the cheapest way for us to get a home. We could save the rent which costs us now 84 dollars per year. We could live with that for quite some time. Foodstuffs are not as expensive here in Edmonton, if we buy it wholesale. Flour costs 3 dollars now for 100 pounds, and clothes and shoes are as cheap as in the States. As far as meat is concerned, there is a lot of wildlife here, pheasants and deer and moose. For you and the children the climate is much better here. Especially for you in general, because you are anaemic. You would be considerably better off here. We should consider that you come here for the time until next spring. I cannot give you an address yet, because I don't know where I will find work. I am going for (?).

Greetings to all,

John Klee

* * * * *

Clive, October 11, 1914

Dear Wife and Children,

Your letter was received from which I see that you are still not feeling well. I am sorry to hear that, but there is nothing I can do to help. How long will this go on until you will have it behind you? I see from your letter that you are not much concerned about a homestead, and I think that this is the only hope I still have to have a home. The way we are now cannot go on for long. I am getting older and cannot always work for other people. Working for ourselves would be different. I believe to have employment until November 15. Then I will go and take a homestead, and I plan to build a house this winter. Otherwise I would have nothing to do during the winter. And when you will be sixty (?) next spring, you could come here to me. And I know that you won't regret it, once you are here, and live cheaper and we'll have a home, so I can still go and work next summer. If I stay here until November 15, I shall have about 200 dollars and deposit here at a bank whatever I won't need to buy clothing for you and the children, and I will save.

With that I just close. My address is still the same.

Greetings to all of you,

J. Klee

33

I HAVE NO way of knowing who supported us. In retrospect, I feel Father was still providing for us. Mother did some home nursing; I recall that "Mrs. Klee" was the one you would naturally call for that need. An incident I remember when we were in the lower grades was when our neighbor, Mrs. Burns, was very ill. The doctor had called and gone (back then the doctor came to the patient; today the patient goes to him, even by ambulance if need be). Mother had taken all four of us to Mrs. Burns' home, seated us around the kitchen table and admonished us to keep very quiet. The patient died that night. A relative had come before morning, but was too late to see her mother alive.

Mother also carried a line of household needs in and around our town. Her intelligence could have taken her far had she realized her potential and been given the opportunity to follow avenues open to her. She was an avid reader. I remember the many papers in our home besides the *Wilson World;* they were from Germany, New York, Pennsylvania; also Christian periodicals, for church was important to her. She did a great deal of writing also. After Sunday dinner, she would sit at the library table (as we called them then) surrounded by letters to be answered or referred to. I recall letters from New York, Stuttgart, Nurtigen, Grünbach, etc. Some we could read — others were foreign to us and, of course, at that time the topics of the day were not important to us.

 34 

WE HAD NEVER considered leaving Wilson — perhaps we were just waiting from day to day for news about our father — even hope that he had been found alive and well. As the old saying goes, "One will grab for a straw when he's thrown into the water." Although there did not appear to be any communication between our parents any more, and though we had had word that our father was missing, we children still spoke of him as if his return as imminent.

We had moved from a $5 a month house to a $10 one that had more conveniences, including indoor toilet — no more chambers under the bed or outdoor privies. I suppose electricity was being put into most of the older homes and, of course, the new ones. One of our neighbors retired, perhaps just getting off the farm and moving to town, and he built a house with two bedrooms for $1,000! So we too were eager for a newer house with modern facilities.

We seemed to be settling into a more satisfactory lifestyle, although I don't know how, except that Mother was working on her two sources, more nursing and orders for home supplies.

Since I will be "leaving Wilson" on the following page, I include here a happy recollection that happened many years later in Wilson. When we were returning from Colorado by car, we stopped in Wilson for a Coke. I struck up a conversation with a nice lady who was serving us. I said, "May I see your telephone directory, please?" She answered, "Of course, and the telephone is right there by the counter." My reply was, "Oh, no, I don't know anyone here. I lived here during my school years and left in 1919, just wondered if I would recognize any names in the phone book." She looked interested now and asked, "What is your name?" I replied, "I am Joanna Shively now. I was Joanna Klee when I was in school." She smiled and said, "I am Ella Whitmer. I was in your class." I did not recognize her, even with that much help, and I'm sure she could have pondered forever and not have recognized me. She had never left Wilson.

 35 

IN 1919, DURING summer vacation, sister Elizabeth and I found jobs in the Midland Hotel, just across the street from the Union Pacific Depot in Wilson. I, of course, would not question the wisdom of this. If Elizabeth said, "Joanna, come on, you can do it if I can," the question was settled. No one could have had a more influential sister than I did. And I think her judgment was usually right. We liked what we were doing and made many friends.

During those days, many factory representatives, promoters and salesmen traveled by train. There were numerous cars on the road by 1919, but were not reliable as they are today, and some would balk at the foot of a hill. I remember when the occupants would give a big sigh of relief when the car made it to the top. Sometimes the passengers would walk up to avoid being stranded in the middle of the incline. I have known of very heavy people feeling obligated to lighten the load.

Back to the hotel — Elizabeth and I became acquainted with some of the "regulars." One was a young man who stopped frequently in Wilson and took a dinner and overnight stay. Now and then his wife accompanied him. We were always delighted, and she seemed glad to visit with us. As we exchanged our backgrounds, etc., she became very interested in us, almost the "godmother" type, who felt she had a responsibility to see this thing through. I recall her frank but sincere statement, "You girls don't belong here all of your lives. These people's interests are very different from yours. They are here to work the land from one generation to the next." (I have been told that the Wilson area is known as the Czechoslovakian center of the United States. I don't know if that is true, but there were a great many names that could prove it to be a fact.) We had made many friends, and as Mother said, "They are just good hard-working people who came over to make a living — not to be supported."

Our friend, the salesman's wife, advised us to look into the possibility of attending Strickland's Business College in Topeka, the Kansas capitol.

As I said before, my sister had started to school one year older than was conventional. Her health was always a problem in her young years. I was a year too young for first grade, but for convenience we started together. She was my mentor through public school. She was also my best friend. We were inseparable but shared a few mutual friends. Elizabeth was an avid student, always determined to excel. Of course, her grades were somewhat better than mine, but she kept me at the books and made me an average or better student.

We aspired to attend Strickland's immediately after graduation, but upon seeking advice, we learned we could forego the junior and senior years and go right into business classes at Strickland's if we could pass their entry requirements. We would be missing some of the sports, but the ball games, football and some girls' athletics, had not been part of Wilson High School's curriculum yet. They were included shortly thereafter. An entry examination precluded all other plans. Immediate funds were required, and our Uncle Fred in Pennsylvania was our angel — glad to make the loan. He wanted his sister's children to have the same opportunities that his other siblings' children were getting.

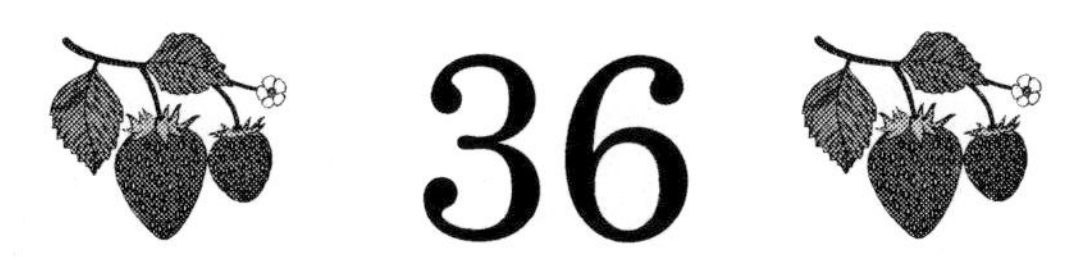

36

THERE WERE MANY plans and preparations to be finalized, but no doubts about what we were doing. We knew we wanted to try our wings. We knew we had some very well educated and outstanding people in our background, so our enthusiasm was understandable.

The outcome was that in the fall of 1919, the Union Pacific Railroad dropped us off in north Topeka. We carried our baggage across the Kansas River bridge to 7th Street — then two blocks to the right and there was the YWCA. We were on our way, very hopeful and confident. The world was ours to explore and conquer!

The salesman's wife, who originated this change in our lives, was acquainted with the Capitol City, where to go and what to avoid. She said the very first thing to do is check in at the YWCA; "they will be eager to help two young ladies unfamiliar with the outside world." (Today, the airlines will put a youngster from the Middle East into the care of a stewardess and fly him or her to the USA or elsewhere.)

The "Y," as we called it, was just three blocks from the school. We moved in and loved it — almost like a college dorm, and just two blocks to window shopping. In this era, the big department stores were in the center of downtown — not miles away along the outskirts of the city, as today. We were delighted with the big stores — Crosby's, Pelletier's, etc. Our funds were limited, of course, but "we can dream, can't we?"

We probably had never been farther away from Wilson in the nine years we lived there than perhaps to Salina to the east, Hays to the west, and I remember going north to Lucas in a car; there was no place to the south that I recall. We could go to Hays and Salina by Union Pacific Railroad. In Lucas we visited the Garden of Eden made of concrete. All the animals were there when we saw it, but I have been told that this spectacle has deteriorated since its creator is no longer there. Somehow the apple tree was wired so that one could hear the Biblical voice speaking.

Lucas has the distinction of being the very center of the United States. Before there were cars, there was only the railroad which missed Lucas and the Garden of Eden by 11 miles. As a girl I did not realize how remote we were from activity. We would not have stayed there as adults; no wonder Mother was unhappy, so far from her many relatives in the eastern part of the United States.

 37 

THE Y.W.C.A. IS a wonderful, safe and helpful stop for young immature women making their first flight from the nest. Topeka's "Y," as we soon learned was the usual moniker for Young Women's Christian Association, was exceptionally well set up for all our needs. There was room on the second floor for dozens of women at one time. However, everyone was supposed to consider the stay rather temporary, as it was popular with girls coming from small towns and knowing no one. They could also have small jobs at the "Y."

On the first floor was the large reception area and admittance desk, a large living room for company, an adjoining reading/study room and a cafeteria at the back. Some of the girls worked in the cafeteria to stretch the loan they had committed themselves to. Elizabeth and I were naturally frugal and accepted any opportunity to benefit ourselves.

One day when I was waiting for some advice at the admittance desk, I heard the lady in charge say to an entrant, "Well, you can have the room for a bit less if you would like to help in the cafeteria now and then or do something on this floor." The girl left and turned toward the cafeteria, and I jumped into the interim between the moment at hand and the girl's return. I said, "I can dust — I'd like to do that for a while if you let me try. That was my job at home." I guess the lady thought this 15-year-old kid should have a chance anyway. I stayed with the job until I found a more remunerative job at Adam's Brothers Printing Company all day Saturday and also at a Five & Dime just a block away.

Everything was going well. We had made friends in the "Y" and joined the fun part, including the swimming pool in the basement where classes were taught for any women's groups that were interested.

But I learned one of the best lessons I could have hoped for and that would benefit me all of my life. Some of the girls had discovered a ladder to the roof of the building, the opening being a trap door. I really don't remember how many girls innocently joined the group who went up there to smoke. I just remember I did go up the ladder. It was fun seeing the city a bit better and feeling important with those girls who were just a little older than I. But when I saw the girls smoking, I realized I was in the wrong crowd. Naturally I did not have any cigarettes, so I had a good excuse for not joining in with what was the reason for being up there. Someone handed me a cigarette and tried to give me my first lesson — how to light it, inhale and blow out the smoke. I tried all of these things, but I added swallowing the smoke instead of blowing. I coughed until I could hardly catch my breath, and the tears came down until I couldn't see. I wanted to leave so badly, but the girls were so busy smoking that they didn't notice or maybe did not care to help me when I tried to pull up the trap door. I raised it a bit and let it drop on my middle finger. It awakened them from their reverie, and they helped with the door as I wasn't doing very well with my injured finger.

I had to suffer alone for I did not want Elizabeth to know where I had been. That was my first and only cigarette, and I am glad I had the experience with it that I did. I might have become a heavy smoker that would not have allowed me into my 100th year on July 21, 2003.

38

STRICKLAND'S BUSINESS COLLEGE was located on the south side of East 8th Street and less than a block from Kansas Avenue, Topeka's main street through the business district. The small college was the stepping stone and springboard for high school graduates in and around Topeka for those who wanted to continue their education, but could not afford Washburn University.

We took a quick entry test and passed. We were eager students, taking all subjects that they would allow at one time. There were times it seemed that we had "bitten off more than we could chew," for we were always available for part-time or weekend jobs, just so they coincided with our school hours. I clerked in Woolworth's Five & Dime on the northwest corner of 7th and Kansas Avenue, just two blocks from school and the same distance from the "Y." It was on this little job that I learned one of the most impressionable lessons we all run into at some time or other, that "you can't trust everyone." Woolworth's dressing room was in the basement of the store. We hung our coats there and put on the little sleeveless garment, identifying us as clerks. I was shocked to hear two clerks discussing how much money they had stolen that day. I felt that this should be made known to the supervisor, but decided against being the one to report it — just hoped that they would be caught some other way. Perhaps the lesson I learned when I was six came into play, concerning the pin on the neighbor's pin cushion, when I was so embarrassed and didn't want anyone to talk about it.

Sister Elizabeth cashiered in a large restaurant/cafeteria, Voight's. It was on the east side of Kansas Avenue between 6th and 7th Streets. We were always available for babysitting, too. The world was great! Everything was working out for us!

39

ELIZABETH IMMEDIATELY EXCELLED in bookkeeping and accounting and later went on to get her license for bank accounting. I chose the stenographic course, shorthand, typing and simple bookkeeping. To this, I added an English course by correspondence.

As soon as they accepted my application, I worked a few hours on Saturday mornings at Adam's Brothers Printing Co., on the northwest corner of 7th and Jackson. Later it turned into a full-time job. But I soon sought greener pastures, which I found with Topeka Title and Trust Co., on West 6th Street. It was satisfactory for a while, but I needed to spread my wings and look for greater horizons that I knew existed out there. Topeka Title & Trust Co. offered me a raise, but I declined.

Almost everyone's goal was to work at Santa Fe General Office at 10th and Jackson. The state capitol, just across the street from Santa Fe, was popular also with aspirants for better jobs. But benefits were not as good and, of course, the opportunities to travel were very alluring.

I became closely acquainted with a family in my church, Grace Episcopal Cathedral. They were August and Josephine Wahl and their three young daughters. Mr. Wahl had recently left Santa Fe for an executive position elsewhere. He knew of a position recently created in the time and watch inspector's main office. He recommended me. I applied and was hired shortly thereafter. Benefits were numerous and generous. Medical care, regular hours and, of course, free traveling expenses were paid a limited number of times each year. This was a new and exciting experience, in the near-new ten-storied white glazed brick building.

It was great fun to take my first trip to Colorado Springs and Denver, with my ever-ready companion, sister Elizabeth, who managed to arrange her vacation to coincide with mine.

Of course, we wanted to take part in everything there was to do, including joining a large group in a hiking trip to and from the summit of Pike's Peak. We started from Manitou Springs. I don't remember how many started, but at the half-way point our group had thinned to less than half. At that point the cog train came along; it stopped, and the conductor called to us: "Girls, you had better get on here. It gets much steeper from here on, and you will be losing daylight." But we wanted to say "we did it," so we refused the offer and kept walking.

Soon we lost some more climbers — they knew a short cut, making the total trip eight miles instead of nine. We had started at 7 a.m. and made it to the top at about 4 p.m. We were among the few that finished and the only girls. Of course, we had to spend the night in the bunks provided for the stubborn few who needed them. The breathing was a bit of a problem, as was the eating. Next morning Elizabeth said, "Oh, for a cup of anything hot! Let's see what the snack shop has." When we got to the dining room's little table, we found they had only rolls and coffee. The coffee steamed but wasn't hot — the altitude was just too high. We also found a group of college boys lying asleep around the pot-bellied little stove. They had walked up during the night.

It took half as long to walk down, but the down trip left more memories and scars than the going up, as my shins were constantly being pushed against the shoe laces of my hiking boots — I had criss-crosses on my legs for weeks.

People go to the top to see the sunrise. That morning it was cloudy, so we didn't see the mountains in New Mexico that are visible on a clear day.

Chicago was another destination we could make — see a stage play and get off the coach back home, just in time to check into my job on Monday morning. Our passes were interchangeable with other railroads; therefore vacations and holidays could take us all over the United States and southern Canada. Train travel in the 1920s was preferred over automobiles which were not as trouble-free as today, also more difficult to operate and keep in good repair.

Sister Elizabeth had also secured quite a nice position for one so new to the large institutions. She became assistant to the administrator of Christ's Hospital, now known as Stormont-Vail in Topeka.

We felt we were doing the ultimate in seeing the world, and we were, as our traveling privileges included some ocean trips off the coast of Maine and other eastern states.

40

OUR FAMILY HAD moved to Topeka by this time, and after settling our obligations to our dear uncle, we bought a six-room frame house on Roosevelt Street off West Sixth Street. It was heated by a coal-fed furnace in the small basement. One large grate between our living and dining room heated the downstairs; the two small bedrooms upstairs were pretty cold, getting just some warmth through the stairway that led up from the kitchen. As I recall, few bedrooms were heated in those days. That would have required a heating unit in each bedroom. The rich often had fireplaces in their big bedrooms.

We were happy to be together again, for we had always been a close family, or so it seemed for a couple of years.

But winds of discontent were blowing around some of us. Our mother, who never liked living in the central United States, and brother Bill, now grown to manhood, were eager to make a change again. This they did very quickly. They were interested in the wide-open spaces in Oklahoma. That move we never understood. But plans were made with hardly a chance for Elizabeth and me to protest. My poor mother was probably looking for another Grünbach near the Black Forest in Germany or a Strawberry Hill in Pennsylvania.

Our mother and brother left us, hoping to do better elsewhere. Bill had not finished school.

I don't remember how much time passed before we had a letter from Hinton, Oklahoma, a small town of 1,300 people, about 60 miles west of Oklahoma City. I was naturally concerned about my family, so I took a weekend trip by train to visit them. Sister Elizabeth and I always worried about our unwell brother, John, and hoped he was given every opportunity he could handle. Brother Bill was a handsome and sturdy young man. No need for concern there.

But we were troubled. Someone must have painted a very false visual picture. My family had settled on a small farm, surrounded by others in similar condition — run-down buildings and land that looked most unproductive. Bill had often had older, fatherly friends from whom he learned to be the handyman he had become. So he was not dependent in that area. But he could not "fix" the land. They were not discouraged at that time, and brother John seemed to enjoy life and was glad to see me.

I was not very satisfied with my visit, as there didn't seem to be the possibility of improving my family's status quo.

The Oklahoma venture was not successful for our family. It was probably too impulsive a move — not taking into account my deteriorating brother, John, who would need more and more care — not just the attention the family could give, but regular upscale treatment not available in the town of Hinton, Oklahoma. Brother Bill could see there was no future for him; he wanted a different life. Actually, he wanted more education somehow. I always wondered where the money was coming from, since I was supposed to believe our father had died. All the years of searching had revealed nothing. Various suggestions were made — one most likely to have happened was that in high water Father went out on the logs to help avoid a log jam.

Elizabeth's and my correspondence with Mother was not very loving — we felt the mistake was Mother's — not ours. She could have had all the work she wanted in the home nursing she did so well.

I do not know how long the family remained in Oklahoma. They did come back to Topeka eventually, unbeknownst to us. Mother probably learned quickly that the house was occupied by others than family, and hesitated contacting us.

41

IN TOPEKA, WHERE I lived from 1919 until 1930, so many things happened on West 6th Street. It was probably the main east-west artery at that time. It was also the route to the State Hospital, later called "Menningers," a nationally known and respected psychiatric clinic. When we first moved to our home in that neighborhood, I was embarrassed to say, "I take the State Hospital streetcar to go home." It was foolish, as we didn't go there — only the streetcar did. The hospital was at the end of the line.

West 6th Street seemed to have more than its share of events, not always catastrophic, entailing loss or sacrifice to someone as in this case. A new addition of land had been opened to the public, especially prospective home buyers. Our home was just a block away in the opposite direction across 6th Street.

I was standing in our bathroom combing my hair, when a very loud explosion occurred. It was very loud! The window was hung from hinges and happened to be slightly open. The blast blew the window violently against my head, stunning me somewhat. Had the window been shut, not locked, the greater force needed to open it would have slammed harder against the side of my head. I had a black-and-blue face for quite a while, but I was fortunate. A child and a small dog were killed. Parts of the little dog were scattered around the area.

This account also took place on West 6th Street. I had walked the short block to our streetcar stop. Several people were waiting, but the streetcar did not come. Soon we all became concerned. I was always eager to be at my job on time, so I didn't wait long — just started walking the 20 blocks, hoping a car would soon come along. Soon there were many people walking. Then we smelled smoke. As we neared 6th and Harrison, we found ourselves roped off. The fire was in the big First Methodist Church on 6th, with the very high bell tower sticking out of the top. Firemen were everywhere, trying to keep the crowd back, aware that when the big iron bell dropped there would be debris and sparks flying in every direction. I had about four more blocks to walk, so I did not get to see the spectacle made by one of Topeka's worst fires and the bell dropping into the inferno. We learned the fire department had run out of water to fight the fire and streetcars could not run through the ropes and barricades.

Ironically, quite some years later, Topeka's most beautiful church, Christ Episcopal Cathedral, was completely burned out inside. Those two churches were just two blocks apart. It was especially sad for me, as I sang those impressive anthems there. I was also married there.

In the early 1920s, at the corner of West 6th and Lindenwood, I saw a huge crowd gathered and in a happy mood. An open vehicle was there and men were hustling around, doing things we did not understand. We soon learned that we were going to hear something by "radio." And we did. Everyone cheered when they heard the first "squawk." It was my first radio reception.

Before long, boys were trying to make them out of oatmeal boxes. My brother Bill was one of them. They didn't get programs, but they were happy to get the encouraging squawks and squeals.

Sister Elizabeth and I missed the last streetcar one night — there was one thing to do — walk home. We had walked from Lane Street west several blocks, when we realized a man had been just behind us for several blocks. We would walk faster, he would walk faster — we would slow down, he would slow down. At midnight, this was something to be concerned about, for we were still a long block from our turn. We never knew if he was following us with bad intent, but we felt we were lucky there were two of us.

Enough about poor little West 6th Street. When I go to Topeka, I still like to go out to Roosevelt, off 6th. I reminisce about how things were, and how they have changed. I hardly recognize most of it — no streetcars, just buses, small businesses deferred to big ones, and some of the houses no longer there.

 42 

THERE ARE PROBABLY still people living today who remember the flagpole sitters of the 1930s. All those I have seen have been on quite tall buildings. The one we could watch without obstruction was on a ten-story building roof at Tenth and Kansas Avenue in Topeka, Kansas. We could watch from our office on the tenth floor of the then Santa Fe general offices, about two blocks away in a diagonal direction. The sitter was a man in a kind of seat hanging from ropes. We were told that he stayed up there day and night, rain or shine. I guess it was high enough to get plenty of wind to dry out his clothes after a rain. The only person tending the sitter looked like a woman with a bucket. The onlookers assumed she had an all day and night job tending to his needs. Food and drink had to be sent regularly, and also a bucket for other uses! One would hope that there were two buckets.

I have never heard or don't remember whether the sitter was advertising or trying to win a bet or contest of some kind.

After a while it wasn't news or of interest any more and the show was over. We heard, without corroboration or disagreement of any kind, that this type of advertising was outlawed. I don't know why it should be. Maybe the man was disgusted with everything around him on the ground, and flagpole sitting was a way of getting away from it all. At least he wouldn't have a hands-on competition up there. Not a bad idea! But I would need to add an umbrella or a parasol and a good book.

43

THE EXACT FEW years that the Dance Marathon was most popular in Topeka I do not recall, but I can guess; I'll say 1924. It took place in the east side of town in a park area. It was an endurance contest with quite a nice gift for the winning pair. There may have been an admittance charge for onlookers, but it seems that it was supported or even sponsored by merchants in the area trying to lure more shoppers from the downtown stores.

Quite a large area was cleared for a circular dance floor; the center was decorated with lights and shrubbery — quite attractive. Music was various dance recordings of the then popular tunes. The whole setup was enclosed in high wire fencing, so spectators could watch entrants easily.

Elizabeth and I went as spectators only. It was referred to as "getting pretty rough." I saw enough of it to agree.

We arrived there when the many dancing pairs were doing very well and were still on their feet, enjoying the applause of the spectators as their favorite pair finished another round.

After the gentler warm-up tunes of the music loudened and the velocity increased to where the now tiring participants could not keep up, the scene became funny or sad — however one felt about it. A pair or two may have dropped out by this time, gathered their belongings and left in a disgusted mood.

After another 30 minutes or so, you would see couples showing signs of fatigue — she trying to rest her head on his shoulder and he doing some strange, irregular things with his feet. Most likely you would see numerous couples stepping out of the race. Some would probably make another lap around, hoping to see those in front falling to their knees.

In another 30 minutes you would see him trying to stumble along while he is actually dragging her on the floor in a stupor. If she is big and sturdy, she may be dragging him!

We never knew who won. We would not have known them anyway. It seems this competition went on another summer or two, but then was outlawed as barbaric activity.

44

WE ALL NEED to discard, for various reasons, things made from cloth. As I mentioned before, worn-out linens were used to make pillow cases. Some of the cutest curtains I ever had were made from the good parts of a matching sheet and pillow cases. They were white with yellow flowers. I sewed the metal rings on and slipped them onto a rod. Several times I heard, "Where did you find those curtains? I've never seen any like them." That was better than selling the partially worn linens for fifty cents as they would do in a garage sale today. We had to conserve during the depression years, and most people became quite adept at using everything.

We all used tablecloths and lunch cloths, also cloth napkins, as paper ones had not come into our homes yet.

The quilt makers used up any new material that was at least as big as a nickel; also, some that were pretty well worn.

Many of us had what we called "rag rugs." They were made from material that was ragged — that even had holes in it. You could cut long strips almost any color, then sew the ends together and add it onto that large ball you were getting ready to use. Some of the strips were braided — then sewed together for a round or oval rug. A cousin in Philadelphia made one over a period of many years; she used hers under her beautiful old dining room table. She used small scraps to make hot pads for the covered tureens hot from the oven.

Old or outgrown clothes always had a use. I have seen crazy quilts, not made for beauty but for general use. When there was just nothing left to a heavy garment but a few patches here and there, those were cut out and made to fit in somewhere in that quilt you had started. Those old warm and wooly scrap quilts were perfect for those bedrooms without heat of any kind, and you still see them today in garage sales.

As frugal as people were way back in the 1930s, we did not sell our cast-off clothes, etc. If we had absolutely no use for them, we gave them away, sometimes to the unfortunate poor and sometimes to friends and relatives. Of course, they could not be compared with all the clothes on racks at garage sales today, some of which look like they have never been worn!

 45 

IT WAS SO much fun, without much expense, to make Christmas presents for friends and family. Of course, the small children were always thought of first, and their gifts were toys and other ready-mades. But for adults we spent less money but made some very utilitarian gifts.

Some of the simplest and much appreciated gifts were the kitchen tea towels. It could be a simple outline of a cup and saucer, teapot, plate or group of flowers, made with embroidery thread in the corner of a tea towel or a decorative stitch all around the hemline.

Another favorite was the pot holder. You had many ways of demonstrating your skill and using up scraps left over from dressmaking. You could put a loop made from bias scraps onto one corner so it could be hung conveniently near the stove. An extra protective pot holder could be made from heavily quilted material about 6" x 12", folded in half, then stitched together on three sides, leaving one side open to slip the hand into. It was dandy protection!

An apron was another popular gift item. It was a bit more work. You could make it as plain or as fancy as you pleased. Flowered yard goods were nice — it was already decorated. I used a piece about 36 inches long which was folded in half and cut out in a half-circle near the selvage. This made a round hole for the head to go through; then cut out two circles for the arms and bound the whole thing with bias tape. You could sew on two narrow pieces already hemmed and attach it to make a tie in the back. You would trim off a bit for the slant of the shoulders and sew together. No buttons, hooks or snaps!

Some of us made lunch cloths, hot roll covers, cushions or sofa pillows. Of course, during the First World War we knitted heavy socks as gifts. The yarn was thick and spongy for our soldiers who were in extreme weather over there.

I really believe that these gifts were appreciated more than the high-dollar gifts we put on our credit cards today.

46

I ENJOYED MY job and also became interested in numerous activities. Singing in the church choir and concerts was my favorite avocation.

The organist and choir director of Christ Episcopal Cathedral kept his large choir "stocked" by listening to small choirs in rehearsal and inviting those who appealed to him to join his choir. He was also a voice instructor. He offered private lessons if I would be a "regular." I often grasped an opportunity to do something different, as I did this time. The cathedral had the greatest of the great acoustics in large churches. It was delightful to try to send my voice to the highest rafters!

Mr. Barnes, the instructor, wanted me to take part in the Marian Talley Contest, which was held in Kansas City, Missouri. I did that, but, of course, did not win. One of the most exciting things I ever did, however, was singing just two phrases opposite the tenor from the Chicago Opera Company, whom our conductor had hired for a concert.

For three consecutive years, I was part of a quartet made up of George Greenwood, bass; his wife Pat, alto; a tenor from First Congregational Church, and myself, the soprano. We sang a 30-minute request program at WIBW, on the tenth floor of the National Reserve Life Building, at 10th and Kansas Avenue in Topeka. The wages were small, but we had a good time doing what was asked of us. Also, it was a great way to make friends and please some unfortunate people who probably had few wishes granted. Some would call the station repeatedly for the same favorite songs. They were so grateful.

We really needed more than 30 minutes for our program, but I needed to grab a roll in the coffee shop and hurry to work.

Mr. George Barnes, the choir director and organist at the beautiful Grace Episcopal Cathedral in Topeka, gave me many opportunities to sing solos and become less fearful of an audience. I must admit that I suffered considerably from "stage fright."

Most opportunities were church programs or in the city auditorium. The most unusual one was at the State Fair Grounds. It was called the Night Show, and in this particular year the theme of the presentation was the Old South, using those old tunes and words we all knew. It was not a difficult spot to fill. My part was the singing — not the acting. I could definitely not have substituted in that area.

One part of the evening's program that could not have found substitution in Topeka was a pair of adagio dancers who had to have a great deal of skill in turning, lifting and balancing, done while slow tunes were playing. The dance team was made up of two men and one girl. One of the men tossed the girl to the other man a shocking number of feet across the stage. She was safely caught at every presentation, but I wondered how they ever learned to do that dance without mishaps.

The girl was very pretty and had a beautiful but scanty costume. The men were handsome, muscular guys. I admired the team very much until the program was over, and I heard the obscene language in the dressing room. There was barely a little curtain to hide behind while changing clothes. It didn't bother anyone but me — they were used to it.

After the last night's program, we were supposed to meet at the specified restaurant downtown for a farewell meal. I hesitated somewhat but did join in. "When in Rome do as the Romans do" has to be applied sometimes. The generous check I received made it all worthwhile.

 47 

IT WAS ON a Sunday afternoon that I had a date with a new friend, also employed in the general offices of the Santa Fe Railway, as I was.

It was very warm and quite windy, just a typical summer day in Topeka. I had been to church as usual. Henry (not his real name) picked me up. Henry was not driving, but was with a young married couple that had a typical car of that time — front and back seats, open but no side curtains. It may have had curtains at one time, or they may have been folded and put into a little compartment in the car.

Cars did not run as fast as they do today, so I could manage to control my wide-brimmed floppy straw hat in the gentle wind. I was wearing a new ankle-length voile dress that I had made. It was of cotton in shades of indistinct tan stripes and with tiny floral design scattered here and there in small quantities. New dresses were not acquired for every occasion as is common today, so I felt really well accoutered that day, in a new dress.

We four enjoyed each other's company, chattered and visited areas in town that we knew — then went over the river to North Topeka and east a few miles to Perry where a lot of roadwork had been done. They cut through some small hills to make the new road flatter, but they left quite large banks with small green trees here and there.

We hadn't noticed the change in the clouds back of us until there was a sudden gust of wind with a few sprinkles. The driver sped up some, but the storm was upon us. With no side curtains we were helpless. Of course, our clothes were soon soaked and my hat was drooping lower and lower. That concerned me greatly until I realized the wind was moving the car. We were definitely in a tornado, soon proven when a small evergreen tree on top of the bank beside us was uprooted and tossed into the air before it fell.

The two men were doing their best for us, but there was simply nothing to do and no place to go for shelter. We were lucky that we were not in the path of various kinds of debris. My dress was ruined but could be restored. Hats cannot be restored. We were lucky we could turn the car around and drive back the way we came rather than driving east trying to find the next bridge over the river.

It may have been a disappointing day, but we had much to be thankful for. The tornado did not create vast destruction, but I hope it is the worst one I'll ever be caught in.

48

NOW THAT I am 98 and the object of my story has been gone for many years, I may confess that I had an idol in the congregation of my church. He was in the same pew with the same couple, his grandparents, every Sunday. He was a student at Washburn College and later in the University in Lawrence, Kansas. To me he was exceptional in that he seemed like such a gentleman, at least he appeared so, and I have never heard anything to the contrary.

He was very tall, had very dark hair and had such courtesy for his grandparents and everyone else. Such people impress me.

I was very blond — just five feet four inches tall, and not in the same social circle, having to work for everything I ever had, and he had the choice of whatever he wanted to be. He chose a high plateau and arrived there as the number one man in a large building and loan company in Kansas.

I knew he admired me just as I admired him. He was a devout Episcopalian and endorsed and supported everything the church instigated or practiced. He even came to programs the Girls Friendly Society of our church put on now and then — sometimes a dance or bridge party — even a sale. He took me to a movie a few times, but our friendship was never serious.

My suitors were never my first interest in life. I wanted to see the world, but opportunities to acquire the funds for travel were few and far between. I must interrupt here to tell you what my clever little son said about that. "Mom, if a woman who is not married is an old maid, then is a man who isn't married an old butler?" We have had many a laugh about Jack's responses.

No, I did not see the world, but I have seen a great deal of it and am thankful I am in this part of it.

Some people are born into wealth. In that spot they do not need a goal to work toward, for they have what we, the middle class, strive for. How do they ever get the satisfaction of saying, "I made it"?

 49 

HOW TIMES HAVE changed! And nothing more than shopping in a ladies' wear store.

I was looking for a dress and found one I would like to try on. On the way to the dressing room I see another appealing dress on a rack. "I'll take this one along and try on both," I said. Some clerks would say something like, "I'll come back and get it after you've tried this one." I suppose I looked like I would put one outfit into my purse? Anyway, she would obey her instructions and should be commended for that.

She helps me put the dress over my head, fastens the snaps or buttons, and I step out of the dressing room to a long mirror. If I meet the owner of the shop, he might push for the sale a bit by saying, "That looks wonderful on you," or, "It looks like it was made for you." At this time I am thinking that I really don't like it very well. So off it comes and I reach for the other dress. Mercy! They must have had this one in the store for a while — it still has snaps below the left sleeve instead of the latest thing they call a "zipper."

The clerk picks up both dresses and says, "I have another dress you might like — just wait in here — I'll get it for you." This goes on for at least an hour; I have decided on something entirely different than I came in for. That decision calls for a different shade of hose. The clerk showed me several new shades and runs her hand partway into the hose to show how they would look with my legs in them. Thank goodness, they are the new kind called "panty hose" where you don't need a garter belt and there is no seam down the back — it was impossible to keep that seam straight all day.

Now I'll need some gloves to match. The clerk chooses several shades keeping all but one pair carefully protected under the glass counter. She tries on several shades, although I am the one who would be wearing them and paying for them.

It wasn't too difficult to exchange a purchase, but nearly impossible to get a refund. Refunds for sale items were not given at all.

Today's "help yourself" methods do make more work for the store help, getting things back on hangers and putting them into proper places, but it makes many more satisfied customers.

People allowed the courtesy of taking home and returning for a refund should also reciprocate by having the garments in extra neat condition instead of thrown into a sack helter-skelter. In our men's wear store we even had a man's shirt returned for refund with a soiled neckband. It had definitely been worn. Now what could be done with a second-hand shirt? We were not in the second-hand clothing business.

 50 

50

AS LONG AS I can remember, the most outstanding thing in Gage Park in Topeka was the swimming pool. I learned to swim in the Y.W.C.A. pool, but I was there such a short time that I probably didn't learn much more than the dog paddle. We did go swimming with our dates, but I never liked getting my hair wet and then having to do something with that curly wet hair that was hard to comb through. I sure would be glad to have some of it today regardless of the trouble.

The hair was not the most undesirable thing about going swimming. It was the smell of the water at times. It was a large pool and no doubt was kept as clean as it was possible to keep it way back then. I tried very hard to keep my head above the surface of the water even though we all wore various and sundry kinds of swimming caps. Some had straps that tied under the chin, and some had a bit of a ruffle round it. Regardless of that, our hair was always pretty well soaked, and I did not like that messy feeling.

There was an even bigger pool across the bridge in North Topeka. We could get over there easily by taking the streetcar on Kansas Avenue. We did not see any of our friends and acquaintances over there, so our trips to the North Topeka pool were infrequent. Who did I go with? Sometimes with a date, but more often just a group of girls. I didn't like the smell of the water over there either and wondered if some of the swimmers forgot to use the restroom before stepping into the pool.

Our dates usually took us to a show followed by some ice cream. We had a few toppings like vanilla, chocolate or strawberry in a dish or just ice cream in a cone. I remember one night two couples of us were somewhere around Topeka Avenue and 22nd Street South. We had been to a show in downtown Topeka and decided to try the new place in South Topeka. We sat in the car to eat our treat. We all agreed we did not like it. After a bit of talk about it, the guys took our cones and theirs and threw them up against the side of the building. I could never join in with pranks, as I was very ashamed of what was done.

So you learn from the episode that there were always pranksters around. No harm was done, but it just wasn't funny and I did not join in with the laughing as bystanders did. The new place probably became defunct very quickly.

 51 

ELIZABETH AND I found ourselves in somewhat of a dilemma. Both of us needed to make a change. Elizabeth's job required that she live in close proximity to the hospital. We had relied on the streetcar, easily accessible, but not instantly available when an emergency case was brought into the hospital two miles away. We probably could not have relied on it much longer, as streetcar tracks were being replaced in many parts of town.

Like most families at that time, we had one car only, and it was now in Oklahoma. Without brother Bill around, the car would have been useless as we girls had not learned to drive. In the early 1920s, most cars had to be "cranked." Some strong women learned quickly to handle that and became adept at avoiding the crank handle as it flew backward. There were many broken arms before the self-starter.

Elizabeth took a small apartment near her job. She was the night-admittance person, handling the desk work. At least one problem was solved.

I had never lived alone any place, so was certainly not willing to live in our house alone, with all the responsibilities of a coal-heated house. Natural gas was being used for heating by this time, but in very few homes. Regardless of that, I still would not have wanted to live by myself. We were hesitant about selling our house, thinking our family might want to return to Topeka.

So we rented our furnished house, and I took temporary room and board with friends in our church. They were eager to have me share expenses in their home. We had not recovered from the 1929 stock market crash, and the Great Depression of the 1930s was already being felt. Many people were becoming concerned about their jobs.

My paternal grandmother, circa 1850.

Farmhouse where my mother was born in 1871, Grünbach, Germany.

Relatives' home and farm near Black Forest, late 1800s.

My parents, John Klee and Pauline Knauer, March 1901.

Tauf-Schein

geboren den

ist am

Im Namen des dreieinigen Gottes getauft worden.

Taufpaten waren:

welches hierdurch bescheinigt wird.

Lasset die Kindlein zu mir kommen und wehret ihnen nicht

My baptism certificate in German. Richmond Hill, New York

My sister Elizabeth (right) and me, ages 1 and 3, 1905.

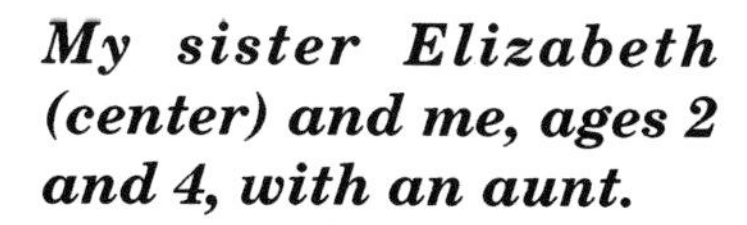

My sister Elizabeth (center) and me, ages 2 and 4, with an aunt.

My first trip to Colorado Springs, circa 1920.

Cog train in Manitou Springs, Colorado, 1920. Elizabeth and I are in the second row; she's on left.

Trip to New York. Myself (left), Elizabeth (center), and cousin (right).

Vintage touring car (left). A friend (below). Manitou Springs, Colorado, 1920

(Right) My sister and best friend, Elizabeth.

Grace Episcopal Church, Topeka, Kansas, where I was the soloist and also got married. It is a beautiful church.

Santa Fe Days parade float, Topeka, Kansas. I am far right, age 19.

(Left) Ada Admatta Shively, my husband's mother, circa 1935.

(Right) I found this photo that my husband, John, took in France during WWI, circa 1914.

John M. Shively — dapper, suave gentleman, circa 1929.

This picture appeared in the **Topeka Capital Journal** *in 1924. I was 20 years old and the featured soloist at Grace Episcopal Church in Topeka, Kansas.*

Elizabeth (left) and myself on the steps of our house in St. Joseph, Missouri, 1932.

Typical Canadian fishing hut of the 1930s.

Easter Sunday, 1939. Marilyn, Nancy and Sally in coats and dresses that I made for them.

Jack, Marilyn, Sally and Nancy holding pet rabbits, Warrensburg, Missouri, 1943.

Ad for our store in downtown Warrensburg, Missouri, 1946.

"Miss Valerie Knauer (left) and her parents, Mr. and Mrs. Wilhelm F. Knauer, of Torresdale, welcome guests to a dinner party at A Man Full of Trouble, the historic mid-18th century tavern they restored." This is my cousin, Wilhelm Knauer, and his wife, Virginia. Virginia headed the Division of Consumer Affairs under President Nixon. *(From the Philadelphia* Sunday Bulletin, *September 5, 1965.)*

(Right) My home for 36 years — 340 E. Market Street, Warrensburg, Missouri.

(Left) Double wedding ring quilt made by myself and daughter Sally. We won a ribbon at the Piecemakers Quilt Guild in Springfield, Missouri.

52

FOR SOME UNKNOWN reason, I did not succumb to the measles epidemic as most young children did when the disease was prevalent in the area. I waited until I was 25 years old, and no one else I was associated with was a victim of the epidemic. I was very ill for two weeks and bedfast for most of that time. Complete loss of sight in one or both eyes, or at best, impaired vision, were the aftermath feared, so I was kept in a darkened room during my recuperation period. I had a very high fever (we didn't have the fever fighters in the 1920s that we have today).

When I had fully recovered, I was tired of being housebound. No wonder I accepted the invitation of a friend to make a foursome by taking the only blind date I ever had in my life. I was wearing the fraternity pin of a medical student in Lawrence, Kansas at the time. I surprised my friends and myself by my duplicity. Right or wrong, the blind date was John Shively, one of the young men who came to Topeka with the Henry L. Dougherty Natural Gas Company. I saw him a few times before his transfer to St. Joseph, Missouri. My medical student had gone to his Bethlehem, Pennsylvania home for the summer. Apparently it did not concern me greatly, as I dated others occasionally. We did not consider the pin an engagement.

John Shively called, wrote brief letters, and came to Topeka frequently, visited some of his friends that he had worked with, and visited me. Then somehow on April 10, 1930, we became engaged. I sent the fraternity pin to its rightful owner, and before long made plans for our marriage. Elizabeth was always my best friend, so my decision to marry and leave her in Topeka was a big hurdle for me. At the time I had not been told that she was also planning to move to Kansas City. Elizabeth dated some, but that was not her number one interest in life. She wanted to be in some kind of business or service.

John Shively and I married in Grace Episcopal Cathedral the following November. I was given the honor of having Bishop Wise (a close friend) perform the marriage service.

We took our honeymoon in California, after surviving the worst snowstorm on record in Colorado at the time. Most roads were impassable as far south as Flagstaff, Arizona. Our car had a rumble seat, but our belongings filled that space, and there was no way to cover it. A couple of boys hitchhiking wanted so badly to crawl in some place. We just could not take them, and wondered if they were among several who died.

There were deaths due to unheated cars and the severity of the storm so early in the season. Snow plows had difficulty getting through. In several places the cars would drive across fields to get to the other side of the large drifts on the highway.

We continued our journey west, going southwestwardly whenever possible. We reached the ocean eventually, considerably behind our schedule. This part of our interrupted schedule did not bother us greatly, but we were eager to get back to St. Joseph to our little rented house which we hoped to decorate for our first Christmas together.

53

IN DECEMBER OF 1930, one of the worst acts of revenge or punishment that could happen did happen near the town of Maryville, Missouri, about 35 miles north of St. Joseph. This was such widespread news that I feel I should interrupt my story by inserting this horrible crime — and the outcome.

It was mealtime — I don't remember if it was lunch or early dinner that I had prepared. After an hour of waiting, I called Louise Crank, the wife of another man in my husband's office. Paul, her husband, had not come home either. We waited until after sunset. John, my husband, had quite a story to tell when he finally arrived. He didn't seem like himself. No wonder!

Several days before, the teacher in a small rural school near Maryville had been raped and killed in the schoolhouse. We made a drive up there the following Sunday afternoon. The schoolhouse was not locked — it looked like nothing had happened as we entered the vestibule, but when we walked to the two rows of seats, we were horrified. Blood was spattered all over the aisle between the rows of desks. I am sure we did not stay there long.

We learned later that the teacher probably stayed longer than usual that particular day to do some decorating for Christmas. The red and green stenciling on the blackboard attested to that. If there was a struggle or screams, no one knows — it is too horrible to dwell on. The man in the farm family with whom she roomed and boarded was immediately under suspicion. He said he expected to be the first to be questioned and was not angry about it. Of course, the whole community was up in arms about such an incident in the quiet little country area. Perhaps they even questioned the older students, for the boy who spoke up said that one day he had seen a dark man standing back of the big tree close to the building.

I don't know how long the search lasted or how he was captured, but they did jail the man who was brought in. Soon the jail was surrounded by a mob, threatening to blast the jail open if necessary to get the suspect.

Perhaps there were not enough police to hold back the crowd, but they did get the suspect. They took him out through the stubbled cornfield by the school, barefooted in December. They managed to get him to the top of the arched roof of the school, chained him fast and burned the building. John, who would have stayed at the edge of the crowd, I feel sure, said that the poor man waved his hand when his pleadings were useless.

I have been told that this happening has been put into book form and can be found in some libraries. Like my daughter said, and I agree with her, "I hope they got the right man."

Ironically, a short time later — just weeks, I think, another girl was caught as she left the streetcar at the end of the line. Again, I don't remember the details. The culprit was caught and hung from a tree on the public square in Maryville. Tension was very tight around St. Joseph and Maryville. "The Murders" were on everyone's mind and made people fearful.

 54 

THERE WERE MANY unpleasant experiences in my kitchen — some downright failures. This one turned out well.

Shortly after our return from our honeymoon, my husband's supervisor advised us that he was sending out a big Christmas present. How delightful!

But the present was a turkey. I was aghast, of course, but it was plucked, so I thought I shouldn't have a problem with it. I would cook it in our beautiful new gas range that my husband had bought from his company. I was eager to try it. But upon examination of the bird, I found it had been dressed only — not drawn. I was helpless — almost in tears, but it was a task that had to be faced and handled.

I eagerly resorted to my helper, "Catering for Two," which provided the step-by-step "know-how" for drawing, cleaning, stuffing and cooking my first turkey. I believe it was the most information I had absorbed in any single day, up to that time. It really turned out well, but I have wondered ever since, and really do not know, what I did with all that turkey. There were ice boxes in 1930, but I doubt that we had one in our partly furnished little house. Those were the days when the housewife hung a sign in her window, telling the ice man how big a chunk she wanted that day. He would chip it off his block, give the waiting children in the neighborhood the chips, then carry the rest of the big chunk on his back into the back door.

This reminds me of the way we managed to have ice in the warmer weather, back in our Strawberry Hill home in Pennsylvania. The ice block would be stored in what we called our wash house. It would be covered with sawdust. I never learned how that would keep it from thawing.

55

MY HUSBAND WAS eager to be the host at the table in his own home, "just for lunch," so he invited his supervisor, not knowing if it met with my plans. He simply called, and I took it from there.

I consulted the little cookbook, "Catering for Two," a wedding present from a foresighted friend. The simplest of "simple lunches" in the book was creamed tuna fish on toast, plus a salad or vegetable, and some kind of fresh or canned fruit.

When our guest arrived, I was struggling with the cream sauce for the tuna and the seasoning for the green beans. The dear man came right into the kitchen, all 260 pounds of him. He tasted everything and told me just what to do (I heard later from his wife that he was still doing that at home). I was not offended, as he would have seemed at home in anyone's kitchen. I don't know if he really enjoyed the lunch, but he ate every bite of it to prove that my effort was a success, I suppose.

I learned later that one thing my husband disliked was canned tuna fish. From that day on we never had it again, except many years later for our children's lunches, occasionally.

We spent many happy times with the supervisor and his wife, Mary. They were our friends as long as they lived.

56

AS WE ADVANCED into the 1930s, the Great Depression years, money was getting scarce and so were jobs. Even the well-educated, with degrees to show on an application, found it impossible to join the work force. Soup kitchens were set up to relieve the situation, especially in urban areas, where there was no yard or bit of land to use for growing a few vegetables to lessen the food costs somewhat (I think of the Irish who had only potatoes to eat for seven years; they apparently survived unscathed).

I remember frequent knocks on our back door made by men eager to work in exchange for a meal, and probably embarrassed to be seen begging. Some preferred money, but we thought unfavorably of that and do not think we ever assisted in that way. We usually provided some kind of satisfying meal, whether earned or not. I don't recall any kind of welfare program as we have today, but surely there was some kind of help in St. Joseph.

I was not very happy in early married life, for I was used to being around people, on my job and at church. I took part in music whenever I was asked.

In St. Joseph, the nearest streetcar was several blocks away, and I had not gotten acquainted with downtown stores. By that time we had a radio, but it belonged to my husband and I did not want to meddle with it. Television was quite some years away in 1931. When the wife of John's supervisor, Mary, heard about my dilemma, she called me every morning. We shared many experiences over the years.

 57 

DUE TO HARD times generally and perhaps harder ones ahead, I became interested in canning food for our pantry when people with gardens had an excess and were glad to sell some of it. Naturally, no one could guess how long the depression would last — it is well that we didn't know it would plague us clear through the 1930s. My friend, Mary, knew the art of canning. So we bought peaches, green beans, tomatoes, etc. in late spring or early summer when gardens were producing more than families could use.

Fifty cents would buy a bushel of various things to be canned. For that fifty cents the seller could buy what he couldn't produce, like flour, sugar, coffee, etc. We traded with each other any inexpensive recipe we found. I think that was the era when casseroles became popular: a bit of ground beef, pork, chicken and even cheese could be combined with cereal, rice and spaghetti to make a main dish. Today when we are enjoying good times and there are jobs to be had for almost anyone, casseroles are still the most popular recipes in the household magazines.

In case I would forget this comical thing later in my story — here it is. My husband loved taking the grocery list and doing the shopping. He did a good job, but I didn't know what to do with a few "extras" he would buy, like pickled pig's feet and baked heart ("just bake it," he said). And once he even bought kidneys for kidney stew. I have seen a recipe for the last dish but have never made it.

My husband, John, grew up in northern Missouri with quite

a large family. His mother learned to cook, bake, preserve and can just about everything the farm produced. John liked all those jars full of food, and I think he would actually have liked for me to fill the cellar shelves like his mother did. But times had changed and I could never have taken on such a responsibility and still have assisted in our various businesses.

One of the things John liked was mustard pickles — great big whole ones. I had seen them in his mother's home in the early years of our marriage when his mother was still canning vegetables from her garden. I made them just once. There was no boiling involved. The big cucumbers were packed into a huge jar — mustard, sugar, salt and a white powder of some kind were added. The lid was put on lightly. After several days his mother added vinegar and some spices and adjusted the lid tightly. The pickles were best if they were allowed to rest quite some time before eating. John loved them — the children didn't like them, so I never made them again. I could never relish that white powder that floated around those pickles. I thought I had done something wrong, but John said, "That's the way they are supposed to look."

 58 

IN SPITE OF our frugality in cooking and every other household expense, times were hard for salesmen in my husband's company. They would sell the small gas appliances that were making their way into our homes, along with the big items like furnaces and heaters. Up to that time, wood, coal and oil appliances heated our homes. When you could see a rather dirty, battered trap window in the foundation, you were looking at the coal chute into the coal bin in the basement of the house.

As the depression worsened, many people wanting to purchase gas furnaces were unable to due to fearing loss of jobs and not finding another, for there were many lay-offs. Appliances were being returned in large numbers where payments could not be made. The trend followed through to the salesmen. So we too found ourselves in somewhat straitened circumstances at times. Many small businesses could not survive and closed, at least temporarily.

We were fortunate. So far husband John was still doing well enough in sales to make our living expenses, but when one is not the "head man," uneasiness is bound to plague one, day after day, wondering which of the team would be dismissed.

59

BY EARLY FALL, we had another member in the family; a beautiful little baby girl was born on September 10, 1931. We named her Nancy Joanne — the first name was chosen by her father and the second by her mother.

I know it is unbelievable, but true, that we paid the Missouri Methodist Hospital in St. Joseph, Missouri, just $40 for the delivery and care for mother and baby for 11 days. That was the usual charge at the time. The long stay in the hospital was to avoid repercussions of any kind. The many infection fighters we have today have cut the hospital stay to way less than half, but the cost has increased many times over for reasons I don't understand — it just follows the trend of accelerating the cost of everything. Of course, our babies are worth much more than the cost of bringing them into the world.

Eleven months later, on a hot August day, Nancy Joanne won the $10 prize in St. Joseph's baby show. Ten dollars was a big prize in the Depression year of 1931.

Author's comment: upon thinking it over, I have decided we should not have "Baby Shows." All babies are sweet and precious. Can you visualize the judges saying, "I think this one is the prettiest." Another one saying, "No, this one has prettier hair," or, "I like the one with blue eyes better." Try to imagine the feelings of mothers whose babies did not win. I remember a man who claimed to have won a prize at the fair for being the healthiest baby there. The last time I saw him he looked like he was competing with the Sumo wrestlers for weight. Final comment: "All babies are sweet, precious, and all are winners."

60

HAND-OPERATED WASHING MACHINES were on the market in 1931 when my first child, Nancy, was born. But the 1930s Depression was well underway, and we soon found out that household necessities cost more than we had planned. Laundry equipment was a real need with a new baby in the house, but we just couldn't stretch John's monthly check far enough to buy a washer. I had seen my mother at times washing a few pieces on a washboard. So we bought a washboard and a small washtub; also a piece of clothesline, and a post to nail a hook into, which required a hammer and nails. All that expense for just washing a few diapers!

Washing cloth diapers was not bad, but it was really hard on the hands. Mother had pretty nice hands, so I decided there must be a trick to it that I had not learned. We solved the problem with a round suction piece on a pole, which was plunged up and down in the suds, and then the rinsing was done the same way.

You can be sure that a washer was the very next thing we saved up for. It should have preceded a radio, a coffee table, a fancy ash tray and a very nice newspaper holder and numerous items we could have done without for months.

In retrospect, I must say I'll take the cloth diaper any time for use at home, rather than fill up the landfills with plastic throw-aways that are creating a real problem in heavily populated areas. The babies would prefer the soft cotton, too.

61

WE HAD OUR second child, Ada Marilyn, on October 31, 1932. This was a bit sooner than planned, but she was a delightful addition to our family. She grew up to be a very talented girl in many, many ways. Anything she could do with her hands was interesting to her. Sewing, painting, sketching or anything artistic was her "cup of tea."

I must interrupt the chronological order of my story to bring in a special account of Marilyn's efforts in sewing. Marilyn started making her own skirts and blouses at age 11. Peasant blouses and broomstick skirts were the young girl's rage at that time. Some readers may not be acquainted with the construction of these skirts — actually using the broom. There were several ways of doing this. Here is the method we used.

We sewed the skirt onto the waistband, using material wide enough to make a full "swinging" skirt. Then we rolled the somewhat dampened garment into a long roll that reached from top to bottom. The next step is giving the roll a twist, as if wringing water from it. Then wrap the garment around and around the broomstick, rather tightly, and fasten or tie with a string. It makes some extra "quirks" here and there. Let dry completely. Now it is ready to wear with your peasant blouse. Today, of course, you can buy the material already "quirked."

It may be interesting to know that for toddlers to about three or four years, I could make a little puffed or cart-wheel sleeved dress from one yard of material, for 15 cents. Compare with today's prices per yard; get an even greater shock when looking at ready-to-wear little dresses today.

I would even have a few scraps left over for a little quilt block. That is the way those beautiful quilts got started. Now they are shown in exhibits everywhere, not only in the United States, but overseas as well.

My daughter, Sarah (Sally, as she is always called), is into handmade quilts, in a big way. She has made prize winners; they are hand-quilted, of course.

 62 

IN MAY OF 1935, my husband was offered the position of manager of the New Business Department of his company, in a different city. It would mean a move to Warrensburg, Missouri, and the surrounding new territory was to be piped for natural gas. We were expecting our third child in late July. He decided to accept the promotion, and we needed to look for a residence in Warrensburg immediately. We moved on July 5th to 314 East Market Street, the only house available at that time. It was not very satisfactory.

Sarah Louise was born August 7th at home, as the Warrensburg Clinic looked unsuitable to me, after the big Missouri Methodist Hospital in St. Joseph, where my first two babies were born. Sarah Louise followed in my footsteps, in that she was supposed to be a boy. I was third also in order of my mother's babies; my parents wanted a boy having had a still-born boy; then a baby girl, Mary Elizabeth. Our Sarah Louise was a beautiful blond, curly-headed little baby, and very welcome, as I hope I was (she was my steady companion for all of her pre-school years).

After just two months' residence on Market Street, we found a house at 420 South Holden Street, a freshly decorated four-bedroom home just two blocks from Central Missouri State College, later known as Central Missouri State University. The Laboratory School, within the teacher's college, was going to be handy for us as our children became preschoolers. But our residence on Holden Street soon became unsatisfactory. The rooms — in fact, the whole house and yard, were planned on too small a scale for our growing family. The folks living there before us must never have opened the door that led to a windowless room under our front porch. My husband decided to open the squeaky door, just wondering why it was there when it was not needed. He used his flashlight and was greeted by hundreds of roaches of all sizes and shelves of jelly jars, some broken, and various creatures running in every direction. He quickly shut the door and ran to consult the yellow pages under "Homes for Rent." He thought the small boards and trash had been there since the house was built. I would think some tenant's curiosity would have led him to open the door. On the other hand, perhaps he did, and moved out fast, as we did.

Another search for a home had to be made. We found a nice house at 315 East Gay Street. In it, the rooms were large, and the neighborhood was made up of older, well-kept homes. We always regretted not buying this house, making a few changes and planning to make it our permanent home. We could have bought it in 1935 for $3,300! Hard to believe today. It could have been converted into two nice apartments later, when we would need less room.

We went by that house many times afterward, wishing we had made it ours.

63

WHEN WE MOVED from St. Joseph, Missouri to Warrensburg, we made new friends very soon, especially John. The smaller the town is, the sooner you know lots of people. In fact, in a town of 10,000 or so, you soon know everyone if you are in business.

My husband, John, was a Shriner, but changed to the Elks Lodge in Warrensburg, as that was the most active lodge in town.

We soon met very nice men in the Elks. They had many social events throughout the year — it is a great way for wives to get acquainted. Unfortunately social groups serve alcohol.

I know that I am in the minority when I say, "No, thank you. I'll just have a Coke," but that has been my choice all of my life, and I don't think I have missed anything by refusing a mixed drink at a party. I have heard, "Oh, come on, Joanna, have a good time," so often that I really did not like to attend parties any more. My husband enjoyed the lodge people, so I did not want to keep him from socializing.

Likewise, the smoking habit did not catch up with me either. There have been many smokers in my family — both men and women. All we need to do is read the statistics to learn if cigarettes are good or bad. I am so proud of my girls — they stopped the cigarette habit and are happy they did. My son may still be smoking; I don't see him often and don't ask him by phone or letter.

When I read articles written by knowledgeable people, I learn that the non-smoker is in danger as much as the user, if he is in the same room. I have cleaned slatted window shades in our home and found that they were covered with smoke residue. What a thought! You can't be buying new shades all the time, and slatted shades don't wash well. The answer is: "Don't allow smoking."

64

THERE PROBABLY ARE not many people in Warrensburg who remember this incident in either 1938 or 1939.

It was in the morning of a school day when I had just Sally at home with me. My husband called and said, “Get ready, I am coming to pick you up. I want you to see something.”

Sally and I were ready very quickly, and I hadn't been told what we would see. We went to “Candyland,” a little ice cream parlor on West Pine Street. There were small round metal tables and the little twisted metal chairs. And there were a lot of people, nudging a bit, to get a better look at the attraction. A quite large young man was sitting at one of the tables, and an older man, who we soon learned was his father.

Mr. Stewart, who was a friend of ours and who had a nice shoe store in town, came over to where I was standing with Sally and said, “Come on, Sally, I will show you the biggest man you ever saw.” He took her by the hand and took her over to see Robert Wadlow, the tallest man in the world. He was eight feet and nine inches tall. He represented a St. Louis shoe company and was visiting many stores.

Mr. Wadlow as not excessively fat, just a huge man. He had trouble standing — several men had to hold down one side of a table, while he supported himself on the other side. I can't explain what it was like to see him towering above everyone — hard to believe. His father traveled with him in an ordinary sedan. Robert simply “folded” and sat in the back seat alone. Robert did not live long — just 24 years. He died from an infection that would not heal, we were told.

 65 

IN THE SPRING of 1939, I realized that there was going to be another addition to our family. It was unplanned and unexpected at a time when rumors of the United States getting involved in the war in Europe were the topic of the day. My pregnancy was a concern to us, of course, for no one could foresee how our involvement could change our day-to-day living. Restrictions of various kinds were already being made on commodities we depended on.

Luckily, the months of pregnancy passed without problems, and a beautiful baby boy was born on January 31, 1940. We named him John Wayne, not after the actor, but to distinguish him later on from his father's middle initial "M."

Now we had four beautiful children to rear and love — Nancy was eight, Marilyn seven, Sarah Louise four and a half, and "Jackie" as we called him now and then, just one month old.

Since the economy was showing a bit of an upturn, we decided it was time to buy a home of our own. We found it the first of March 1940, at 340 East Market Street. It was to be my home for 46 years, with varying numbers of occupants. We were an average family, respected citizens, with the usual highs and lows, blessings to appreciate, and deaths to mourn. I felt really "low" when my unwell brother John died in 1937, and again in December of 1942 when my mother died. She had an apartment in Topeka and was found there, dead in bed. She did not get to see her beloved Grünbach once again.

Mother's death happened exactly one year after the bombing of Pearl Harbor on December 7, 1941. What a day to remember! Pearl Harbor and President Roosevelt's proclamation, "THE UNITED STATES IS IN A STATE OF WAR," did more to change Warrensburg and vicinity than anything before or since. The land a few miles east of us, called the Blue Flats, became Whiteman Air Force Base in record time, and the small town nearby it, called Knob Noster, grew by leaps and bounds.

In our town of Warrensburg, the usual influx of students to CMSC changed almost overnight. Being a teacher's college, there were more women than men in the college; they lived in the one dormitory and around town. Soon the women needed to find quarters elsewhere, as the dormitory filled quickly with Air Force and Navy personnel. There were jobs everywhere pertaining to war preparation. In fact, one was not loyal and patriotic who was not doing something to help. Even renting a room or two to temporary civilian workers at the air base was lessening the great demand for sleeping quarters. We made room for two secretaries from Whiteman.

One area that did not flourish, which, in fact, came to an end very quickly all over our vicinity, was the manufacturing of anything metal. The only thing being done with it was gathering anything — iron, tin, etc., and stacking it on the courthouse lawn, to be hauled to munitions factories. Even children understood this endeavor and were diligent workers.

Soon everything became scarce — beef was rationed, even to restaurants, nylon hose disappeared. Chocolate candy bars were seldom seen; in fact, most confections containing much sugar were unavailable. One of my young daughters heard that some store had received an order of chocolate bars, so she rode her bicycle to town immediately, hoping to be one of the lucky ones. I don't remember if she was or not. Gasoline was rationed. Sunday afternoon rides were unpatriotic. I remember trying to buy a little train set for our son Jack. None were in the stores. They were making some out of heavy cardboard. Cardboard construction of toys did not blend well with the energy of a four-year old who was already interested in mechanical things. There were several scanty Christmases during the early 1940s.

66

AS MY FOUR children were growing up in the 1930s, it took a lot of conserving to keep them looking well dressed. Luckily I enjoyed making all those pretty little dresses (slacks or jeans were not in vogue yet). I even made my son's little pants and shirts.

My girls loved going to Shepherd's Dry Goods Store. Nancy and Marilyn were hopeful that there would be an obsolete pattern book that Shepherd's employees saved for me. They liked cutting out the models, trying various other dresses on them, etc. Another bit of fun was spinning the seats of the stools where ladies sat to look at the pattern books. It was a bit noisy but tolerated by the clerks.

At that time there was still the unique method of making change when a sale was made. There were little containers into which the clerk would place the sales ticket and cash for the purchase. She would close the container and start it on its way by a long cord to the office where change and approval were made. What was the reason? Were the clerks unable to handle cash, or were the owners expecting a hold-up? Anyway, it furnished entertainment for the children. The clerk waited patiently for return of the cash. When it was received, the purchase was wrapped in brown paper and tied with a string.

Shepherd's had a store of well-chosen merchandise, but they did not have a restroom for the public — just for the help. Actually, no store in Warrensburg had a restroom — the only place to go was to the courthouse. I guess we deserved that convenience — that's where we paid for it with our taxes.

Another place that saved an obsolete book for us now and then was the wallpaper pattern store. Our girls really enjoyed making new outfits for paper dolls. It made lots of entertainment, and I believe they learned color coordination from it.

There were many ways to use spare time without spending money, of which there was little in the 1930s. I am glad I experienced that decade of having to make do.

67

MY MOST RELAXING day in the 1930s was ironing day — Tuesday. I had two ironing boards, one that pulled out of the wall in the kitchen and was hidden by a neat little door. This board was used for quick press jobs and was a blessing to my three girls who looked like they were going to a "well-groomed" contest when they were simply going to walk three blocks to school.

My other ironing board was the big heavy kind that opened up easily and was very sturdy. It had priority over everything else as it stood between the dining room and the living room, facing the radio. Everyone was gone until noon when my children came home for lunch. After 1940 when we had our son Jack, he was there with me all day. If he had something to play with that had wheels, he was happy (I should mention here that Jack was telling us the names of cars at the age of three and corrected us if we were wrong).

"Stella Dallas," "Ma Perkins" and "Queen for a Day" were my weekly "guests." They were on the radio other weekdays, I suppose, but I couldn't give them more than one day a week.

I was asked a few times, "What do you give your children for lunch? Mine get tired of peanut butter and jelly." I can't recall that we ever had peanut butter and jelly for lunch. We had creamed hard-cooked eggs on toast — a cheese fondue, minus the wine. We put it on toast. There were numerous macaroni or spaghetti dishes, quickly prepared and satisfactory. We had a sweet simple dessert like Jello, applesauce or pudding if I had time.

This custom changed considerably when we had the Annex Restaurant during the war. I must admit that I was not the kind of mother I wanted to be; I could not be in two places at the same time. Good mothers want to say that their children were number one, but like many others, I simply had a part to perform during the war. People were driving to Kansas City five days a week, leaving the half-grown families to fend for themselves. I was happy to have a bit more freedom when peace was declared and I could be a homemaker again, for a short time at least.

Perhaps I should not mention this unbelievable statement made by one of our neighbors, whose son was too young to be drafted. He said, "I hoped the war would last a long time. I was making more money than I've ever made in my life." Can you believe it? I thought of that remark every time I saw that neighbor and disliked him to the utmost degree.

68

AT ABOUT FIVE years of age, something very startling happened between Sarah Louise and myself (we were calling her Sally by this time).

Sally loved playing with her dolls, loved taking them for a ride in the doll buggy, which had a good path around and around between the kitchen, hall, living room and dining room.

She would say, "You be the mother and I will be the little girl." The incident goes like this: "May I go to Martha's house and play?" I said something like, "Yes, you may go but don't stay very long." That was our game, and I went right on ironing my Tuesday basket of clothes.

All of a sudden I realized that Sally had not made the circle for a while. I called but there was no answer. I searched upstairs, the basement where she never went, then outside, looking over sidewalks as far as I could see. There was no sign of my five-year-old girl or her doll, but the buggy was still at home. After five or ten minutes I became panicky enough to call my husband's office. An abductor could go quite a few miles in ten minutes. John came immediately, not concerned yet. We drove around our neighborhood, becoming almost terrified when we saw a deep excavation, probably made for a water or sewer line about a block from home. We were about to involve the police when we decided to take a side street or two. At the first house we approached, there was Sally and her little five-year-old friend, Martha, on the porch of her friend's home. Sally's request to go was for real this time. Martha's mother had taken her older girl to school and stopped by to invite Sally. She should have let me in on the invitation.

I don't remember if we continued our game, but if so, it was taken seriously every time after that, you may be sure. Today, I would not wait ten minutes before contacting the police, with child abduction being so rampant in our country. I see the many photos of "Missing Children" and realize we must all take part in preventing it, and our laws for punishing the abductors should definitely be tightened.

 69 

A DEAR LADY, Mrs. Sweet, had sole charge of the Laboratory School at Central Missouri State College. She taught our pre-schoolers to use their hands in crafts, crayons, games, and how to mingle with others. Her classes or groups were usually five years old. She helped me by allowing my four-year-old, Jackie, to join her group for a few hours while I tried to fill in the vacancies at our restaurant.

A part of the morning at "school" was used in a walk around the area. On one of these walks, Jackie ran away from the group and simply did not respond to Mrs. Sweet's calling. I don't know how close to town they were when he left the group, but that four-year-old walked into our restaurant, crossing the railroad tracks on the way. Mrs. Sweet could not have left the group to catch him. He probably could have outrun her anyway, as she was not a real young lady. I learned why one usually sees a helper with a group of children outside.

My husband was a close friend of our chief of police, Mr. Anderson, who happened to be in the restaurant — very timely indeed! He asked Mr. Anderson to talk seriously with Jackie, explaining that the train couldn't stop for him. Jackie replied, "Oh, yes, the train will stop for me."

How glad I am that nobody informed us quickly that he was on his way toward town. We would have panicked, I'm certain.

70

WE HAD A little black and white fox terrier. His spots were well scattered over him, so someone named him "Domino."

He belonged to all of us, but I think he liked Jackie best; there were more exciting things to do when he followed Jackie all over town. He even went to school occasionally. He knew the way; actually he knew his way all around Warrensburg. He even went to church now and then, when the church door was left open and Sunday School was in session. He would just walk down the aisle.

One day, Domino was not at the house when everyone else had come home. He didn't come home the next day either, nor the next. When the fourth day rolled around and our pet had not been found, our concern mounted to desperation and tears. I don't know if Warrensburg maintained a dog pound in the 1940s, probably not, for one of us would have thought to look there.

On about the fifth day, I think we had all given up our search, when Mr.. Wilson, the gas meter reader, called to tell us that he had that day seen a little dog deep down in an excavation that had been made for the base of our town's new water tower. He thought the bark he heard sounded like Domino. You see, everyone in town knew Jackie Shively and Domino.

My husband hurried right over to the designated spot, and when he saw that little mud-covered dog (for it had rained) and heard that familiar but weak bark, he knew it was Domino. He hurried back home to get a ladder, for it was much too deep to jump down or get out without help. In a short time we had a cold, scared, hungry, but happy little buddy, wrapped up warmly, with a good meal going down fast. I don't know who was the happiest, the family or the dog.

 71 

WE LIVED AT 340 East Market in Warrensburg, Missouri, during the years that our children were growing up. I believe there were only three houses on the street that were not very old. So we were surrounded by mostly older people. They were mostly nice older people.

The Phillips to the west had no children, and a lady on the west of them lived alone and never married. She had a married sister though, Mrs. Ridge, who had never had children. She and her husband lived right across the street from us. She was very intolerant of children and was the worst kind of neighbor — perhaps just an unhappy person.

Our three girls had gotten new bicycles and had to try them out — down to the end of the street — then back, but on the other side. Mrs. Ridge apparently wanted to live up to her name by building an invisible "ridge" between us (just a pun!). She would actually stand in her yard or steps and wait for the girls to come back on the other side. You guessed it. They purposely made the ride down and back again to annoy her.

This time when they returned, Mrs. Ridge was waiting for them with the garden hose in her hand and actually turned it on the girls with their good clothes on.

I don't know if my husband just happened to be watching, whether we called him, or if he even saw her with the hose.

Mrs. Ridge's sister was married to Mr. Anderson, Warrensburg's chief of police. He was also a friend of my husband and frequently stopped in the restaurant to chat.

John told Mr. Anderson that he witnessed his sister-in-law

sprinkling the girls and took a snapshot of her doing it. That was the last of this episode for all concerned; Mrs. Ridge did not gripe any more so the fun was over. The girls rode just on our side of the street.

Then there was Miss Carver with quite a wide parking on her property. She wanted us to keep our little black and white fox terrier from excreting waste matter on her side. I have heard of people carrying a sack for that purpose, but I would never expect anyone to do that.

We had three boys growing up next door to us. They played ball and threw frisbees, jumped the fence to retrieve their toys. We disregarded it, even though they were pretty hard on the fence.

Surely everyone knows that a neighborhood quarrel never ends once it is started. Time and tide do not dispel harsh words between neighbors; in fact, the trouble grows with the telling.

 72 

WE HAD FRIENDS, the O'Briens, who opened and operated a very successful uniform factory, "Utilitog," in Warrensburg in the 1930s. They had learned the business as employees of a large factory in Kansas City, Missouri. He was Fred and she was Martha. Fred traveled all over the U.S.A., selling his product, and Martha was the designer of the uniforms for men and later for women also.

Our friends knew my penchant for making children's clothes. They encouraged me to look into designing and manufacturing young girls' dresses. The pressure from them, and perhaps the imaginary light at the end of the tunnel, were too strong to ignore. I made a trip to a Kansas City garment factory to "learn the ropes" of the "rag business." I had had no experience with the heavy-duty sewing machines. We were still in a deep state of depression, and there were many jobless people. Even though they were experienced in their trade, their skill was not needed. I knew my changes for a job were slim, but I hoped to break the barrier of the inexperienced by becoming "a poor single woman with four children to support." My old house dress, run-over heels, old hat and dark glasses must have pulled on their heartstrings, for they hired me without any problems.

I soon realized the whole plan of manufacturing dresses was not for me, but I stayed just long enough to learn using the machines, which literally "run away" with garments as they are put through the assembly processes. The experience proved invaluable to us in a later venture.

73

THIS IS JUST a little true story that could have had a bad ending.

We were having our garage re-roofed one day when Jack was about eight years old. I was probably in the house preparing dinner — it was in late afternoon.

I kept hearing someone talking outside and soon realized it was a pleading voice, and there was no one out there but Mr. Miller, the roofer. Then I heard, "Please, Jackie, bring back the ladder." Jackie had moved the ladder away from the garage, and there was no way that middle-aged man could get down. Jackie, I think, was in a secluded spot to see what would happen. He probably could have jumped down easily.

I don't know how long Mr. Miller was up there, but we probably had to pay considerable overtime.

74

JOHN SHIVELY, MY husband, was not selling furnaces, gas ranges, refrigerators, washers, etc. These things all used precious metal in their construction. His job for the duration of the war was to be "hand shaker" and good-will man. This was not to his liking, and he started to check out the situation in our city and the small town of Knob Noster, near the new Whiteman Air Force Base.

There was definitely a need for a larger restaurant, cafeteria, or cafe with a large dining room and a few booths against one wall, which many patrons consider more comfortable. A long counter, soda fountain and ice cream desserts were also a need.

My husband and four of Warrensburg's businessmen got together to look into the possibility of making a "big bundle" of money in the restaurant business. John, my husband, was knowledgeable about such equipment, as it was closely related to the domestic equipment he sold every day.

One by one, the four associates dropped out of the "restaurant business" in rapid succession. Being involved would mean hands-on partnership. They just wanted to invest in it. That left John Shively with a plan, but he knew absolutely nothing about operating the business he hoped to start. That would come later — hopefully. So he went ahead with his first plans, alone.

The remains of a defunct venture, the Annex Restaurant, still had four walls and part of a ceiling after a fire some time in the past. It seemed worthy of being restored, refurnished and reopened; luckily it was right next door to the movie theater. The owner of the building worked well with John, and all of the above happened early in 1942.

The restaurant plus long counter seated 75, as its predecessor did. Quality food was served without gouging the patrons. Following is a copy of the menu. It looks like we were literally giving food away. In fact, at times my husband would use his one "closed" day a week to find enough hamburger, ice cream, etc. to get through the next week.

Keeping full staff in the kitchen and dining room was a big problem. There would be a full crew one day and a skeleton crew the next. Jobs were plentiful and pay was better in the various war plants in Kansas City, Missouri, just 50 miles west. That is where the potential help for the restaurant went, of course. Also, new ventures of all sorts popped up, taking employable people from our town. We were fortunate to have high school juniors and seniors in the dining room and long soda fountain. Some cooks around Warrensburg were eager to make a change, so that spot was usually filled.

The worst experience my husband had was with a potential employee, a young girl he had not seen before, who applied for a waitress position. She had a nice manner, I guess, but was filthy, had dirty feet and no hose or socks. My husband had to tell her that if she would clean up she could go to work. She did not come back. Who knows why? Perhaps she had no place to live. Had I seen her, I might have taken her home and let her clean up, if she seemed to be just a very unfortunate, homeless girl. I'm not sure about what I would have done. I like people, and like to see everyone have a fair chance.

One day I had a call from John — he was desperate. Several employees did not show up — they were kitchen help. could I help out for a short time? No, I did not have food service experience of any kind outside the home. I don't know what I did with three-year-old Jackie — probably took him with me — as there was no other choice. From then on, planning the meals, typing daily menus, which varied according to the amount of meat that was allotted to us, was my task. Many foods were unattainable. Ice cream, for instance, was rationed, and John had to "beat the bushes" to find other sources than our best Franklin Double X.

Keeping things running smoothly in the kitchen was also difficult at times. I was an apprentice on the job as were those I was supposed to guide. Wherever people were working, they kept alert for something better — sometimes they simply did not show up. My husband kept a list of applicants to keep a full crew. Our two daughters, Nancy and Marilyn, helped in the dining room when we were short-handed. They were eager to help, especially when the handsome uniformed servicemen came in. Our pretty daughters were not overlooked by the servicemen from the base; they were a bit young, but who doesn't enjoy being noticed!

We had a nickelodeon at the rear of the restaurant that was well patronized from morning 'til closing time at 10:30 p.m. or so. Two favorite heartbresaking records, "I'll Be Home for Christmas" and "White Christmas," put hundreds of nickels into the player — probably paid our rent. The boys seemed to get some comfort from it.

Comments often passed between us, wondering how many of those boys (and some girls) would see another Christmas over here, and if they did, what shape they would be in, mentally or physically. Jobs should have been waiting for every returning service person, even if it meant making another person temporarily jobless. In spite of everything, the Annex was a huge success.

The following is the menu from our establishment, The Annex. Oh, for a ham salad sandwich for 20¢ today.

Sandwich Selections

Served Plain or Toasted

Ham Salad **20c**
Salmon Salad **20c**
Egg Salad **15c**
Peanut Butter **20c**
Bacon and Tomato **25c**
Olive Nut Spread **20c**
Tuna Fish Salad **25c**
Lettuce and Tomato **15c**

Sliced Chicken **35c**
Roast Beef with Lettuce and Tomato **30c**
Roast Pork with Lettuce and Tomato **30c**
Baked Ham with Lettuce and Tomato **30c**
Gooseliver with Lettuce and Tomato **25c**
Chicken Salad with Lettuce and Tomato **25c**
Peanut Butter and Bacon with Lettuce and Tomato **25c**
American, Brick or Pimento Cheese **20c**

All Sandwiches Served With Potato Chips and Pickle Slice

Annex Club House

Sliced Chicken, Crisp Bacon, Fresh Ripe Tomato Slices, Lettuce and Mayonnaise, Potato Chips, Pickle Slice on 3 Slices Golden Brown Toast

45c

Grilled Jumbo Steakburger on Toasted Bun, Potato Chips, Pickle Slice

15c

Toastmaster

Roast Beef, Baked Ham, Fresh Ripe Tomatoes, Crisp Lettuce, 1000 Island Dressing, Potato Chips, Pickle Slice on 3 Slices Golden Brown Toast

35c

Breaded Pork Tenderloin on Toasted Bun, Potato Chips, Pickle Slice

20c

The Varsity

Ham Salad or Egg Salad, Fresh Ripe Tomatoes, Crisp Lettuce, Mayonnaise, Potato Chips, Pickle Slice on 3 Slices Golden Brown Toast

30c

Grilled Jumbo Frankfurter on Toasted Bun, Potato Chips Pickle Slice

15c

Hot Dishes

Soup (Homemade) **15c**
Chili (All Meat) **25c**
Spaghetti **10c**
Spaghetti with Chili .. **25c**
Chili **20c**

Salads

Potato Salad 15c
Sliced Tomatoes 15c
Fruit Salad 25c
Head Lettuce (choice of dressing) **20c**

Tropical Fruit Bowl

Chilled Diced Fruit Salad on Crisp Lettuce Bed, Banana and Pineapple Fruit Slices, Choice of Dressings, served with Buttered Toast

45c

Vegetable Salad Bowl

Early June Peas, Green Beans, Diced Beets, Crisp Celery, Shredded Carrots, Green Peppers, Shredded Lettuce, Ripe Tomatoes, Choice of Dressings, served with Buttered Toast

40c

Minimum Charge of 10c Per Person for Drinks Served in Booths or at Tables After 5 p. m., Except When Served With Sandwiches or Meals

Fountain Selections

Ice Cream Rationing Makes It Necessary to Use Half Ice Cream and Half Sherbet in All Sodas, Sundaes and Ice Cream Dishes.

Jumbo Ice Cream Soda **15c**

Cherry	Pineapple	Lemon
Strawberry	Vanilla	Root Beer

SPECIAL ANNEX COOLER

Grapefruit Juice, Cherry Flavoring and Syrup **10c**

Melba Peach a la Mode **15c**
Chocolate Sundae **20c**
Fresh Strawberry Sundae **25c**
Pineapple Fruit Sundae **20c**
Marshmallow Sundae **20c**
Butterscotch Sundae **20c**
Crushed Cherry Sundae **20c**
Parfaits—any flavor **25c**
Crushed Nuts on above Sundaes **5c**

Annex Special Sundaes

Hot Fudge Sundae **20c**
Vanilla Ice Cream served with a pitcher of hot fudge.

Betty Co-Ed **25c**
Vanilla Ice Cream with Marshmallow Sauce, Sliced Bananas, topped with Whipped Cream, Maraschino Cherry.

Special Banana Split **25c**
Vanilla or Strawberry Ice Cream, Whole Banana, Chilled Fruit Salad, Chopped Nuts, Whipped Cream, Maraschino Cherry.

The Air Corps **25c**
Vanilla or Chocolate Ice Cream, Marshmallow Topping, Spanish Peanuts, Whipped Cream, Maraschino Cherry.

The Annex **25c**
Vanilla Ice Cream, Crushed Strawberries, Strawberry Ice Cream, Crushed Pineapple, Whipped Cream, Maraschino Cherry.

Malted Milk (any flavor) **20c**
(With Egg—25c)
Deliciously Rich Topped With Whipped Cream

Miscellaneous

Limeade **10c**
Orangeade **10c**
Lemonade **10c**
Phosphate (large) 10c
Orange Juice **10c**
Coca Cola (large) 10c
Milk Shake **15c**
Grape Juice **10c**
Cold Ovaltine **20c**
Orange Freeze **20c**
Root Beer (large) **10c**

Drinks

Coffee **5c**
Tea, per pot **10c**
Postum **10c**
Milk **5c**
Buttermilk **5c**

Setups Not Served for Mixing Drinks

 75 

YESTERDAY THE WAR was raging and killing — today peace was declared.

In our place of business, our restaurant, the environment changed just as quickly and conversation along with it. Of course, we were making money, but in our hearts and minds we were eager for peace in the world. We knew we would miss those dear boys who would come into our place in droves. The train tracks and depot were at our back door, and the boys even used the back entrance like they could hardly wait to get back from a weekend leave. The movie theater was right next door, so they could have a meal with us and go to the theater and get back to the base on time. Some would play the nickelodeon or records after the movie or have some soda fountain treat.

But some of the most hopeful boys would eat bowls full of cooked carrots. They were told that carrots contain what eyes need for good vision, and they were striving for positions as navigators.

A few of those young men, so handsome and well groomed in their uniforms, were such "regulars" that they would take the trouble to say good-bye. Some were sad and some were eager for action.

Our young waitresses were sad, too. They had dated some of the boys from Whiteman Air Force Base — a few had even married them. I have wondered many times if some of them we knew best had survived (many years later a friend of our son Jack, who was a navigator, was reported missing — his body was found in a remote area some 30 years later, with identification still on him).

Suddenly it was over; the boys from Warrensburg who survived came home and our old ambiance returned. The dormitories and classrooms were returned to the girls, and civilian life went on for most of us, although WAFB is still training today in the airfields near Knob Noster, Missouri.

We waited a long time for stores to be restocked to normalcy again. Some jobs became extinct and some new ones were created.

We knew we would not be in food service forever and did not want to be. Peace came abruptly and was certainly welcome, but some of us said, "What now?"

Before long we put our business on the market, and it sold quickly. Now it was our turn to consider the future of our lives and work, but not with fear as did those we served for three years.

With all my heart, I hope the time will soon come when we will find solutions to our troubles between nations and do away with innocent young people being murdered or maimed in battles they did not create.

We do not have our children to be sure we have soldiers to send into battle. We have them to love and help them to live the normal 80-plus years intended for them.

76

AS A VERY young man, my future husband, John, left his home in Braymer, Missouri, to seek his fortune in Kansas City. His desire for good clothes and proper attire generally sent him to a men's wear store, where he was employed immediately. His tenure there was short, as the United States had entered the war (World War I) in Europe, and he was just the right age to enlist or be drafted. He did enlist in Naval Service and was in for 18 months, taking healthy troops over and bringing injured ones back, and some that had paid the ultimate price of war.

After World War I ended and we were nearing the 1920s, John did not go back to the job at the clothing store in Kansas City. Instead, he became a factory representative for a gas appliance company, doing more traveling than he liked. Therefore, when the opportunity arrived, he joined the Henry L. Dougherty Company and was stationed in Topeka. That is where I met and married him several years later.

Now, 26 years later, peace was declared again. It was an earth-shaking day, similar to the day war was declared, except that it was happy instead of sad.

Close to home and especially to our family was the realization that changes in our lives were imminent. My husband's job with the Gas Service Company was still waiting for him after the long leave of absence. John hesitated going back. After being the "chief" for three years, he did not relish the idea of being just an "Indian" again.

We hoped to sell our interim, the Annex Restaurant, quickly, as it would now be less productive for us as population at Whiteman Air Force Base decreased. It had been a very successful business and a good experience.

We were blessed with a quick sale of our restaurant. I had a young family that needed most of my time, and they were entitled to it, after three years of sharing it with the Annex.

 77 

JOHN THOUGHT OF going back to men's clothing business, but needed something more than a clerkship. He wanted a store of his own.

Being free since selling the restaurant, he had time to do some research into the availability of well-known brands of suits, sport coats, slacks, etc. And, of course, a suitable location. A building right in the middle of our main street was about to be vacated, and John was pleased with it.

To make a long account a bit shorter, I will just say that "Shively's Men's Wear" was opened by John M. Shively and assisted by Russ McDowell, a well-known Warrensburg man. The venture was doing quite well, although it was across the street from another men's store. In 1954, John took over and closed out the Dunham Men's Store in the next block south, and moved his store to that location.

Shortly after the opening of our store, I realized there wasn't going to be a time when I would be just a homemaker, which was satisfactory with me. Our tailor became ill one day rather suddenly, leaving pants to be cuffed, waists to be fitted and coat sleeves to be shortened. I took over temporarily; before long, permanently, and enjoyed it.

It seemed there wasn't much change in the style and color of men's clothing — just a change from plaid to plain or stripes, and cuffs to plain bottom trousers, but always white shirts with little more than a stripe. John had barely settled in when a sudden change happened; the "pink shirt with grey slacks" became the rage. We could not keep enough in stock to satisfy the demand. It was a break for John, as he had just suffered the expense of moving. "One good change calls for another" proves to be true here also, as orchid and lavender shirts were the next colors tried. They did not make the splash that pink shirts did, but the "die was cast" — white shirts had to take a back seat from then on. Now many years later, all colors are used, whether they flatter the suit color or not.

78

ONE THING JOHN enjoyed was Sunday afternoon rides into the country, with all four children expressing a personal wish, like taking a little rough place fast enough to bounce them around a bit or hitting a low spot between two slight hills to get a jolt. I am just realizing that that delight has been curtailed for the little folks today because of the seat belt restriction.

My husband's very favorite thing to do was to go fishing — not necessarily big-time fishing — just a good pole and some bait, and preferably a boat so he could seek out those special places where "the big ones" hide.

On a Sunday ride, we often crossed various kinds of bridges, some where you could see the stream through the cracks and the squeak of the old framework made you wonder if there was one too many in the car this time, and you felt a sense of relief when you got to the other side!

Without a pole you could still get out of the car and look down and hopefully see a few minnows swimming around. John really got a thrill from seeing those minnows.

The family, especially our girls, liked getting out of the car and checking on old run-down abandoned houses. It was surprising what could be found — for instance, old letters, pieces of broken dishes or a few old books. In a way, it was dangerous, as that old forsaken junk made a good hiding place for such life as snakes or varmints of various kinds. I suppose that Sunday activity would be frowned upon today. Some places looked like one could fall through the floor — and that could be a real disaster for the predator, as he would have no recourse for injury or could be fined for pillaging.

What we enjoyed most on a Sunday ride was the singing. I have never known my husband to sing except on a family ride when we all joined in. He liked to sing the old Southern songs like "My Old Kentucky Home" and "Swanee River." Those were the songs that everyone knew — today we never hear them any more. Another bygone age.

 79 

OUR TOWN HAD carefully preserved numerous buildings; one is the old mill near the railroad track. It was still operating when we moved there in 1935. When the ownership was broken by death, this very old wooden structure was a problem — too high for ordinary use, and was looking fragile. However, it survived nearly a hundred years of wind and rain.

Our son, Jack, had been given permission (not by his parents) to climb to the top and catch pigeons that found good roosting on that five- to six-story building. The pigeons were given a chance to roost on our garage, but it wasn't to their liking — they left — probably just went back to the mill.

Just recently someone has bought the quaint old structure. We were told the boards will be used for decorating by lovers of antiques. Although I don't live there any more, I wish the faithful, "determined" old building could have been reinforced here and there and included in the town's sightseeing. It is the old things that keep reminiscence going, not the new.

Our son also had a penchant for turtles. At one time, we had 22 turtles of various sizes and of different shades. We had all kinds of "food" and grass on the screened-in porch to make the turtles feel at home, but they were unhappy and made efforts to get outside.

We settled the problem by naming the creatures, writing the name on white tape and placing it on their backs, then releasing them. That way we could tell if they came back; son

Jack watched hopefully, but not one was ever seen again. But just think how much more fun he had and learned about wild life than he would have from watching some of the non-events on television they see today.

 80 

OUR FAMILY HAD a very bad experience in the late summer of 1950. My sister Elizabeth learned that she had ovarian cancer in an advanced stage. Her doctor set her up for surgery immediately and then found her condition as serious as he expected. That was 50 years ago; it makes me wonder if the same diagnosis were made today, would doctors at least try a treatment before the finality of surgery? So many medical advances have been made in the last decade alone.

Elizabeth owned and operated her own ladies' wear business on Wornall Road in Kansas City, Missouri. With the news of her serious illness, she needed help — both during the uncertainty of her recovery and possible dispersal of her business. With family at an age where I could leave them in the care of their father, I stayed with Elizabeth during her recovery period and kept her business open, at the same time trying to prepare for the closure.

We finally did what was our only choice — sold out and had Elizabeth move in with us. She recovered somewhat, but soon was hospitalized in the Warrensburg Clinic, which was not very suitable.

I do not remember where we first learned of the cancer hospital in Oak Ridge, Tennessee, a government-operated experiment station for hopeless cases of internal cancer. I believe our Warrensburg's Dr. Damron suggested that we try to get Elizabeth entered there if she was willing and if there was a place for her. After all, it was experimental, and only a few kinds of the disease were studied and worked on at one time. Doctors from all over the world studied there and took only a few patients at a time and required complete submission of the patient to new methods of treatment. Our chance for getting in was small as there was room for only 25 patients and about 100 doctors at any time.

In a few days we had a call from the Oak Ridge clinic — they had a place for Elizabeth. A group of doctors were there studying the latest treatment. Of course, we were thrilled at a chance for Elizabeth's recovery.

My three girls were about 19, 18 and 15, but our son was not 11 years old yet, and John, my husband, had a business to attend to. The girls and their dad could manage, but Jack needed to live with some discipline and interests in his free hours. My sister was unable to travel except in a prone position which, of course, had to be in an ambulance.

All of these arrangements were made, and on the appointed day Bob Brauninger, a funeral director in Warrensburg, picked us up and we had the long trip ahead of us, with Elizabeth requiring regular medical shots on the way. I was the navigator watching every roadside direction, as Oak Ridge was purposely secreted somewhat from the public. Until about a year before our entrance, every road had had a sentry posted. Since restrictions were reduced somewhat, just one sentry appeared on top of a building just inside the gate. He stopped us with a few questions, and when he saw the ambulance, he asked nothing more.

Mr. Brauninger took us directly to the clinic where we were met with badges to pin on our clothes. They contained a deterrent to the damage that could be done to us by the nuclear experiments, which I do not know enough about to explain. Bob Brauninger left immediately so he did not need a badge; I pinned mine on as told. Jack, a juvenile, could not enter the building at all.

When Elizabeth was settled into her room, which contained

several other beds, I needed to find quarters for Jack and myself. Not knowing that they did run city buses, I called a taxi. The driver told me I might have trouble getting a room. I couldn't understand that as I did not see great crowds of people, but he did not explain further.

At the admittance desk I was told that I would need a reason for being there — that would be as one accompanying a patient, but they would not take Jack. I could possibly get a bed for the night in the women's quarters who were employees in the experimental places, but they wouldn't take Jack. He was too old for the women's quarters and too young for the men's. There was one more chance to get in off the streets — get a job — a reason for being in Oak Ridge.

I went back to the hotel and asked again for a room, promising I would just stay one night. They agreed.

My plan was to run an ad in the daily paper for a room. I bought a paper to learn its name. Something led my eyes to the ads. There was one for a "room for rent." I called and got directions, using the city bus. I found Mr. and Mrs. Mitchell and their big beautiful dog, Pete, that took to Jack immediately. I should say they took to each other for Jack loved that dog, and the Mitchells loved Jack. Surely our Lord arranged this. Like most people in Oak Ridge, the Mitchell family had worked in those life-threatening plants. And like all occupants, they were allowed a house with just enough bedrooms for the family. There were two bedrooms. When they had moved into the house, the Mitchells' son was living with them, but he left the city and his parents had not yet reported that they could now manage with a one-bedroom house. Were we lucky or what!

I now needed a way to pay the rent for a longer period than I had anticipated and to have a reason for being in Oak Ridge. The town isn't large, and I had no idea where or what to try for in a job. The little department store surely had a vacancy some place, or one coming up. I tried here and there and did find that they were thinking of better help in the drapery section. This was about as remote a spot as any store would have, but I took it and watched Mitchell's newspaper for any kind of a "Help Wanted" ad.

I applied and had an interview for the position of assistant to the city manager. I was delighted and hoped to go to work shortly. They would never miss me in the little department store. I have never liked working with curtains anyway.

The result of the interview was, "We will call you if we need you." I was disappointed, of course, for I assumed they were interviewing others. But I guessed wrongly, for they called me in a day or two, giving me the job. Of course, I did not tell them I might not be in the city long. Now I was going to make enough money for room and board for Jack and myself. Also, Mr. Mitchell, now retired and in limbo himself, had a companion to ride around with him, and I no longer worried about Jack riding around on the buses all day, just for something to do.

I went to bed early, wishing to be in fine fettle next day for my job. Once again I hit a blank wall — in fact, a very sad thing happened. Elizabeth had taken a turn for the worse about 4 a.m. I went to the hospital at once. They had put her into an oxygen tent with little hope for a change in her condition. Later in the morning I canceled the job, and much later in the day I joined Elizabeth in the room where they administered the worst kind of treatment. She had begged the attendants to allow me in the room close to her. She was seated on a chair — I was standing in front of her as she leaned her head against my chest. I held onto her hands as they punctured her lung and put in the irradiated substance. I could feel the jerk of her body, although she was heavily sedated some way. I was wearing the badge so was not in danger myself. The wall in this particular room was solid metal for everyone's protection.

They put my sister back into the oxygen tent and I sat with her. Unbelievably, in a few days Elizabeth improved enough that they granted her wish to be taken outdoors in a wheelchair. I took her for a little ride on a beautiful day. Jack was with the Mitchells in good care. Of course, he was not allowed in the hospital. He could only look in through a window in sister's room and wave. They were very strict — made no exceptions.

I was so encouraged, but the staff there said her improvement was very temporary. They had had only one miraculous recovery on record. It was a younger woman from Tennessee who actually appeared to be well again, and was still visiting the hospital now and then to prove it.

Part of my family came to Oak Ridge and were impressed by Elizabeth's apparent improvement. Since it was time for Jack to be home for the beginning of the school year, I went back also to handle necessary duties. Then I would go back to Oak Ridge. Elizabeth changed our plans, however. She actually came back to Warrensburg by herself, feeling very hopeful.

In a very short time we had to put her into Warrensburg's clinic. I don't recall how long she was there, but improved a bit again. During our stay in Oak Ridge, husband John had had our screened porch closed in to make an extra bedroom that Elizabeth could have to herself. She wasted away quickly and did not respond to medication any more. We took turns staying up with her. John had taken his turn one night, when he noticed a decided change in Elizabeth. He called up the stairs for me to come down quickly. I talked to Elizabeth and held her hand. I think she knew I was there, but said nothing, just closed her eyes. My sister and best friend was gone into a better life where puncturing the lung was not necessary any more.

81

ONE EVENING IN 1955, as husband John and I were visiting with friends in our living room, we received a telephone call from a member of the Elks Lodge in Kansas City, verifying that he was speaking with John M. Shively of 340 East Market Street in Warrensburg, Missouri. We did not have as many "troublesome" calls and scams by phone then as we do today, but an unfamiliar voice at 11 p.m. on New Year's Eve was one to pay close attention to, expecting a prank perhaps.

The voice asked, "Did you purchase a raffle ticket, a chance on a car, in Sedalia, Missouri?" John had attended a salesman's showing in a Sedalia Hotel a day or two before. The number on John's ticket agreed with that of the caller, but John still didn't get excited when the man said, "You have won a new 1956 Cadillac, and you can pick it up at Greenlease Motors in Kansas City at any time." It still didn't seem plausible that he would have the winning ticket. After all, jokes and tricks happened on New Year's Eve.

The raffle was a money raiser for the replacing or repairing of the quarters of the lodge, so thousands of dollars were needed, and a raffle might help raise the money.

We had close friends in Kansas City, the Pitman's, so John called them and asked them to call the lodge and call back. Sure enough, there would be a beautiful new Cadillac sedan waiting to be picked up. It was a special New Year's Eve!

 82 

I AM HESITATING a bit about including this in my book, but all you readers know it is good to have a hearty laugh now and then, even though the cause of it was created by a questionable prank. Anyway, here it is — you may censor me if you like.

Our daughter Marilyn, husband Bill and his parents were having dinner with us one Sunday. After a main course of chicken and dumplings, it was time for the dessert. Every cook likes to outdo his skill a bit with a colorful tray of desserts. My husband took part in this in order to make it very festive.

Dinner plates were removed and a vase placed in the center of the table with a beautiful arrangement of flowers. Second cups of coffee were poured and the lights dimmed. Everyone was eager for the masterpiece. Husband John served Bill's father first. It was a "horse dropping" from our neighbor's field with a neat blob of whipped cream on the top! Of course, the rest of us got something else.

Everyone laughed long and loud, including the recipient of the "special dessert," which was quickly removed and replaced with something more delectable.

Husband John and Bill's father delighted in harmless jokes. Another trick was a small balloon under the tablecloth and plate of Bill's father and the cord in John's hand. Imagine the look on the face of the man whose plate moved as the bulb on the other end of the cord was pressed!

Everything was for fun, and it really kept away any chance of a dull meal. Bill's parents were a delightful couple and always had some kind of joke for John, who was ready for anything.

 83 

THE ASSASSINATION OF John F. Kennedy in Dallas, Texas, caused about as much excitement, uproar and confusion as would the beginning or ending of a war.

As we all know, this well-remembered tragedy happened on November 22, 1963. It has been interesting to hear the great variety of places people were when they first heard the news on television.

I was in a hotel in Springfield, Missouri.

My son-in-law wanted me to try my skill or ability as a representative of a new insurance company in which he was an officer. The Modern American Life Insurance Company had its headquarters in Springfield, so that was the place chosen for our classes. I know we were in a hotel on Sunshine or Glenstone; I also recall a long balcony that led to numerous rooms. I was on the balcony and could see many people in the lobby below.

I hardly had time to ask the person nearest to me what was going on. I found out from the voice below. "The President has been shot. President Kennedy is dead." I had a perfect place to see it all — the injured, dying President looking so helpless and poor Jackie, disregarding her finery and trying to help her husband. I remember that little pill box hat that she had made famous, now beaten about a bit as people crowded around literally wringing their hands.

There are ugly revengeful things that just can't be fixed — they just need to be instantly changed. Vice President Johnson changed his title right then and there, even before the damages from the murder were cleaned up. Mr. Johnson must have been in a state of shock, too. From being just a kind of tagalong for many months, he had, in the blink of an eye, the whole responsibility dumped on him — no questions asked. No “maybe he’ll recover” or “we’ll see how he is tomorrow.” President Kennedy died November 22, 1963, and that will forever be the biggest news of that date and year.

84

WHEN WE LIVED on East Market Street in Warrensburg, Missouri, the train track was almost right back of our house. Our big 150-foot back yard and our field for gardening were between us and the trains that went east and west several times a day. I knew their time schedule pretty well when I was hanging diapers on the clothesline. I could hang them wet and remember to bring them in quickly when dry; this had to be done between trains. Those coal-fired engines really put out the soot, especially when the engineer had to give it a little extra power after the stop at the depot just a few blocks away. When the wind was in the south, we would have grey diapers if we forgot to bring them in.

One Sunday when daughter Nancy's family, Julie, Nicholas and Reneé were coming from Topeka and Sally's family, Dana and Robbie were to be there, too, it seemed like the right day for that train ride I had promised the children.

I don't know where the fathers were that day, probably watching a baseball game on television. Grandpa Shively did not miss those very often.

We planned that after dinner the children and I would board the train in Warrensburg and ride to Sedalia just 30 miles east of us. In the meantime, Nancy and Sally would drive to Sedalia to pick us up.

This all worked out as planned. I had descended from the passenger car with my five charges when Nancy discovered Reneé had left her purse on the train. Nancy told Sally to "get on the train and find the purse." After boarding the train to retrieve the purse, Sally soon realized that the train had begun to move down the tracks. Nancy shouted, “Porter, stop that train — stop that train!” The train eventually stopped several yards down the track. Sally ended up getting off the train in total darkness and running back to the platform with the treasured purse. A happy toddler awaited.

Years before, Jack had told our chief of police that the train would stop for him as he crossed the track from school. At least it stopped for Reneé’s purse.

85

MY HUSBAND, JOHN, had been an exceptionally healthy man for all the years I knew him. He did smoke cigarettes all those years — probably started the habit in the service, as many of the young men did when there were few entertainments in their leisure hours. His health did not seem to be impaired from smoking. He enjoyed eating every meal. I have known families where someone would say, "I don't want anything for dinner. I'm not hungry." Only if someone was ill did he or she pass up a regular meal in our home. John really enjoyed eating — a compliment to me.

But one day John surprised me when he said, "I think I should see a doctor." I was not aware that anything was wrong with his health. He did see a physician — one who had spent his first practicing years in the military and had become somewhat abrupt in giving his prognosis after examination of a patient. He said, "You have prostate cancer," and added, "it is probably terminal." The logical next question from John was, "How long do I have?" The doctor gave him less than a year. It was like a bolt out of the blue when John told me. I tried to think of encouraging things to say, but there really aren't any at a time like that.

Daughter Marilyn's husband Bill knew a doctor in his home town of Ponca City, Oklahoma, who was recognized for his expertise and success with prostate cancer patients. Of course, we all felt a bit of hope. Plans were quickly made and carried out. I flew with John to Ponca City where he entered the hospital immediately. After considerable testing, surgery was performed. We were given little hope. I tried to be encouraging, but when John was not even interested in the World Series on television, I knew he had accepted his fate. He was a devout baseball fan.

Bill and I took turns sitting up with John. We never left him alone — I think he knew that we were trying to face the inevitable with him. Bill and I were both in the room when the nurse recognized the final signs. John died on October 31, 1966, which was also Marilyn's birthday. It was like an omen of what was to come, for Marilyn died in a car accident ten and a half months later.

John was taken by ambulance to Warrensburg. He was only 70 years old. With his apparent good health and longevity on his side of the family, it seems he should have lived at least the average years for men — about 79, I think.

John Shively, my husband, died on October 31, 1966, nine days after our last grandchild's birth on October 22nd.

Another sad coincidence was that our daughter Marilyn's birthday was also October 31st. John had been ill throughout the past year, but somehow we always hoped for a miracle. He had partially retired from the store and was hoping to have a few years of leisure, but it wasn't meant to be.

86

ONE OF THE most upsetting things in my life occurred one September morning in 1967. I had not been at work long when the telephone rang. The call was for me from my son-in-law, Bill Eubank, in Ponca City, Oklahoma. He was a naturally jovial person, so I knew almost from his first word that something terrible had happened. His wife, my daughter Marilyn, had been in a car accident and was badly injured. I remember I said something like, "Are you sure it is real bad, Bill?" I was hysterical, of course. He said, "Jody (that is what my in-laws all call me), I am afraid it is real bad."

Everything changed instantly. Our assistant in the store immediately locked the store and took daughter Sally and me to the hospital in Oklahoma City, where Marilyn was in intensive care. Bill's mother and father were in the wreck also. Mr. Eubank's injuries were not as severe as Mrs. Eubank's. One of her feet was badly damaged permanently.

I can hardly recall the shock. I still call on daughter Sally to tell me the particulars of this terrible accident. When I saw Marilyn lying there, I took her hand and ever after have hoped she knew that I was there, even though she did not speak. I could tell that the doctor was not hopeful when he said, "If she survives 24 hours, she has a chance to recover. But she lived four days and then was gone — just ten and a half months after her father. The doctor said, "Head injuries always leave 'scars.' " He said she would never have recovered completely as the blow was so severe — it was the only sign of an injury. I have never asked Bill how many people from the other car were killed, but I know that there were several.

Marilyn's and Bill's little girls were Carrie, five, and Kristi, seven years old. Carrie almost accompanied her mother and grandparents to Oklahoma City. At the last minute they decided to leave her at a friend's home. She could have been another fatality.

I stayed with the distraught father and his little girls for a short time, trying to help make adjustments, but there is no help at a time like that. Bill also had his parents to think about. It was the worst time of my life, losing a beautiful young daughter.

My mental strength was truly being tested to the limit; in fact, it was frayed to the breaking point. I really did not have the desire to go on.

I had always liked going to church and taking part in its activities, but I had never given my life completely to our Lord, so I felt that I had no "asking power" from Him. But I was in desperate need of a "crutch," and believed enough to pray. I prayed on my knees in our living room, hoping to be recognized, though I felt unworthy. I prayed aloud, "Lord, please help me with these burdens. Either let me go into permanent rest or give me a reason to live."

My daughter Sally, realizing I had really given up, said, "I guess the rest of us don't mean anything to you." At that moment I suddenly felt a whole new attitude envelop me. After all, I had two daughters, a son and grandchildren in my life.

87

MY SISTER'S UNTIMELY death in 1951 made me feel like half of myself was gone — we were that close all of our lives.

Of everything that happened, my daughter's death in September 1967 was almost more than I could bear. Marilyn's car accident was so severe that she could not have enjoyed her life again.

The young man who had been with us in the store since his college days was now interested in becoming a partner. When I thought about all those boxes of shirts that had to be stacked in boxes, on high shelves, from a ladder in the store room, the thought of him staying with me became bright and encouraging. But at age 62, how many more years would I want to be going to work six days a week? We soon sought the help of a lawyer, and the outcome, after a few days of considering pros and cons, was the sale of the business. I agreed to stay with him for ten years as an employee, but free to come and go at will. I retired at 72 and immediately planned several trips.

 88 

MY YEARS AT Santa Fe Railroad's general Offices in Topeka in the 1920s allowed me to see most of the points of interest in the United States and off shore in the northeast, but I was ready for places I hadn't been — had just read about.

For no particular reason, a friend and I chose Alaska to be first on our agenda. Fairbanks was to be our northernmost visit. Our trip was in the late 1970s, when it was said "any car driven to northern Alaska and back isn't worth much." It wasn't the smoothest ride I ever had, but I think a few obstacles and inconveniences along the way give one something to remember. No doubt, flying up there these many years later makes for more comforts, etc., but our rough spots by bus added to reminiscences. Why, I remember a stop or two where there was no way to bathe our feet but wash one foot at a time, one on the floor and one in the sink.

Although Fairbanks was scheduled to be our farthest point north, another passenger and I wanted to go to Barrow Point at the Arctic Circle. After watching those little Alaskan planes literally bounce up from the narrow little highway and landing uncertainly the same way, we decided Fairbanks, as scheduled, was far enough to the north.

I wanted daughter Sally to make the trip with me, but she is neither a flier nor a sailor, so our trips together did not leave the continent. A few thousand years ago, before Bering Strait created itself, we could have walked across to Russia, through the Chukchi Peninsula.

 89 

ONCE, WHEN VISITING my mother's cousin, William Knauer, in Torresdale on the Delaware River, a suburb of Philadelphia, he said, "Come on and take an extra day or two. I'll take you in the cruiser right up to the spot where you lived." I wanted to go, but when I left home I promised my husband John that I would be back in time to assist with a sale at the store. Instead of being thanked for my loyalty to husband and business, I was teased and criticized for forego-ing such an opportunity

It really was a foolish mistake. I should have called my husband about an unexpected opportunity to be a guest in William and Virginia's beautiful home on the Delaware. I could have slept in a bed where former Presidents had spent the night and probably have eaten at the table where they had breakfast in the morning. The house was a popular stopping place for politicians and famous visitors, before William bought it. Outside, a bit of a lane led to wide concrete steps used for boarding a vessel.

William took me on a tour of his beautiful house. He showed me a desk formerly owned by James Madison. He was offered a very large sum of money for it, but did not sell it. William and wife Virginia dearly loved and cared for everything in the home, which was sometimes used for political gatherings, campaigns, etc. Virginia was repairing some very old deterio-rating draperies, rather than replacing them with something out of context with the surroundings.

90

WE HAVE ALL heard the old adage, "Truth is stranger than fiction." I have experienced a few incidents myself where this saying was proven.

On my first trip to Europe, my friend Evelyn and I were in a state of keen anticipation for everything we saw or expected to see.

I actually have forgotten in which Italian city we were when this happened. We had walked past numerous shops when we came upon a little eating place. Some alluring aromas were coming from it that caused us to stop and consider taking our lunch there and to try one of those exotic pasta things that they are famous for. So we did just that. We had gotten our food and were enjoying ourselves when I looked up from my plate. I could hardly believe my eyes when I saw a man and woman and two young girls talking with each other, as if they were coming in for lunch. I knew the man to be Dr. Keith Stumpf from our town of Warrensburg, Missouri, our home at that time. He had been an occasional customer in our store, so there was no mistaken recognition on my part. I said, "Evelyn, that is Dr. Stumpf from Central Missouri State University; I can't believe that this could happen. I am going out to say hello and let them in on this unusual coincidence."

Well, I ran out, but not alone. The proprietor of the cafe was running out after me, wildly waving his arms and a towel into the air, and letting off a number of accusatory words I could not understand, of course. He thought I was leaving without paying my bill. I don't know why he did not wonder about poor Evelyn left sitting at the table. I hurriedly tried to explain that I knew the people out front, but he kept right on talking and berating me, no doubt. The Stumpfs were discussing having lunch there also, so perhaps that was enough "salve on the wound" to make up for my apparent attempt at thievery. Maybe if I could have spoken Italian I could have persuaded him to give me a discount on my meal in return for bringing four customers into his cafe!

91

ABOUT 25 YEARS ago, daughter Sally and I took a trip that included Williamsburg, Virginia, and Allentown, Pennsylvania. After checking the map, Sally said, “Mom, we are just a little distance from Stroudsburg that you spoke of. Let’s leave the tour and rent a car.” We did just that — drove to Bushkill and found the exact spot where our house had been.

Our Strawberry Hill had been flattened, the house razed, and the land transformed into a beautiful golf course. The wooded area had been partially stripped of its trees. I recalled a little path where I walked with my mother into just the fringe of the woods. Mother would fill her pan full of huckleberries, as we called them. Today they are called blueberries. Mother had warned me not to go near the old stone fence close by, for she had once noticed a snake lying on the top stone. It was enjoying the sun on a cool day, no doubt.

We crossed over the river to Flatbrookville. We were very disappointed. The rivulet with the little arched bridge seemed narrower, the church and schoolhouse were gone — they deferred to progress, I guess. And the children and teachers were gone.

Am I glad I went back? Not really. I should have kept dreaming about our beautiful playground, which has probably been leveled even more by now.

92

ONE DAY WHEN daughter Nancy and I were walking on a street in Topeka, we met with one of her friends. The friend had an obligation to meet and no place to start.

Her obligation was to find a lady willing to finish the school year as the house mother at the Zeta Tau sorority house on the Washburn University campus in Topeka. The lady that had filled that position had become ill and would most likely not be able to return.

After introductions had been made and the friend learned that I lived alone and was just visiting Nancy, she had the perfect potential house mother! She said to me, "Why don't you do it? You would have your own apartment, private bath, just show up for most meals, weekends off, and a small check; also able to call or see Nancy any time."

There were usually 24 girls in the house. On the main floor there were two large visiting rooms, large dining room and well-arranged kitchen. After ascending a beautiful winding staircase, you could see a large bedroom at both ends of the house, with four beds in each. Several single rooms were across the front, and the housemother's apartment was in the middle at the back. The basement bedrooms were all singles.

I barely hesitated — in fact, I stayed there before final decisions were made. Almost without exception, the girls were very good to me, and they were very courteous and eager to please. Maybe compliments are in order to make the house-mother feel at home, but nevertheless, they said, "You are the best house mom we have ever had." I believed it in part anyway, for they vied with each other when I needed a ride or accompanied them to a program.

I never corrected the girls unless they asked my opinion. I did not allow the male visitors any place but on the first floor. One girl on the ground floor wanted to cut class occasionally so she could sleep, but there I balked. She said, "If so and so calls, tell him (her) I am sick." I said, "Are you sick?" When she said, "No," I refused to lie. She left school before the end of the term.

Most of the girls are mothers now, I suppose. One I heard about is the mother of triplets. I finished the school year and stayed all of the next year. It was pleasing to know that I could get along with these different personalities. Not one of these girls said a disagreeable word to me in the year and a half that I was there.

But that stay was long enough, and it was time to pursue some way to live my final years. Now, here I am at 98 feeling as well as I did in 1980!

 93 

LATER ON IN my life, when I had become a widow and was living alone, I had an opportunity to try out a sudden impulse. At the home across the stret and a bit to the left, a new person was seen going in and out of the house and parking her car in the driveway. I said to my daughter, "Sally, I am going to find out who lives in the Summer's house." I went over and met Charlyne Van Oosbree, who proved to be the librarian at Whiteman Air Force Base. She had four cats, Mrs. Gray, Minnie, Splotch and Zeke. Charlyne was also a widow, as myself, an antique collector like Sally, and a dyed-in-the-wool reader which we are also. We had so much in common. My inquisitive mind resulted in an ongoing 15-year friendship.

It doesn't always work out that way, but it is better to speak up and be rejected than live side by side like two statues in the park, never knowing if there was a common interest between us. I have had many pleasant conversations with first meetings — as in the mall when I am resting on a bench while my daughter is shopping.

I like to bring up the subject of age and sometimes ask them to guess my age. I have had comments like: "I don't believe it" or "and you are still walking!" It does a lot for me and perhaps for them who may look upon old age with fear.

I do not look upon old age with fear, but I may have at some time in my younger years. Now, I like to think about what good I can do before I die to make people happy.

I can recall having had a terrible dislike for someone who was cruel or unkind. So I was doing an unkind thing myself for disliking someone. We can all recall such incidents, I think.

Trying to straighten out a problem in a peaceful way is so much better than a shouting contest, which just causes bad exchanges of words and permanent wrinkles in one's brow. I know, for we have a few, too.

 94 

IN 1995, I was at a crossroad, nothing to motivate me and nothing to hold me to status quo. Daughter Nancy was living in Topeka, our daughter Marilyn's family in Florida and Connecticut, son Jack and family in Wichita, and I was living with daughter Sally in Warrensburg.

Sally had been wanting to move elsewhere for some time. Her son and daughter had moved to Ozark, Missouri, so we visited frequently there and the many delightful places in the area. Springfield is the city close by to the north, and the popular vacation land of Branson to the south, with scenery galore in every direction. So what were we waiting for in Warrensburg? After 60 years we left and have never returned.

I had sold my home several years earlier, so was footloose. Sally was born in Warrensburg and lived there most of her life. It was a good place to grow up with freedom to come and go at will. School friends had scattered over the years, and we needed a change of scenery!

Sally bought a house in Nixa, which is trying hard to meet the city limits of Springfield and is succeeding. At present, it is said to be the fastest-growing area in Missouri. It is adding 200 new students each year to its schools. The temperature is "just right" — a bit warmer in winter, summers very pleasant, friendly people and more casual living. It isn't a Strawberry Hill, but we can do our part to make it that. We love the Ozarks!

I have had a good life and a bad life. I have never been rich nor impoverished. I do not have a college degree per se, but consider myself pretty well educated by experience, many correspondence courses and perseverance. I have had opportunities that I grasped and some I should have. Perhaps I still can!

95

MANY YEARS LATER when I had retired, I was asked once again, "What is the most impressive thing you have witnessed in your life?"

There have been many, but I think I will give my trip to the Holy Land and the Jordan River first place.

I was on a bus tour over there with about 40 passengers from numerous states. One couple that caught the attention of all the rest of us was a pretty young beauty shop operator from California, accompanied by her 86-year-old grandmother. This must have been planned, for everything fell into place.

We were all invited to walk along the bank of the Jordan River. The older lady had changed her attire to a long garment. Shortly a young man joined us. He was wearing ordinary dark slacks and a white shirt. He took off his shoes and led the shoeless grandmother down to the water's edge. They did not stop — just walked right into about waist-high water. He baptized the grandmother and said a beautiful prayer for all to hear. We realized he was a minister. Then he asked for all who knew the song to sing it together. It was "Shall We Gather at the River."

Then we all left, having witnessed a life-long wish of an old lady, to be baptized in the Jordan River. As she walked out of the water, the grandmother said, "Now I am ready to die if it is my time." I have never seen a happier face with tears in her eyes.

96

MOTHER HOPED SHE would get the opportunity to go to Grünbach, Germany once more. Perhaps it would have changed enough to be a disappointment, in which case she was better off with just her memories of the little hamlet near the Black Forest.

In spite of 80 or more years of trying to solve the mystery of my father's death and burial, we have had no encouraging clue. Although I will continue to be interested in grave markers in the British Columbia area where he wanted to buy land, I realize it must be thought of as an unsolved mystery. After all, identification had been sent home — so his body, if found, carried none.

Surely somebody knows somebody who had heard of John Christhoff Klee, my father.

Although our home on the Delaware that we called Strawberry Hill seemed like the ultimate in scenic beauty, close proximity to Mother's siblings, I have learned we can make our own "Strawberry Hill" anywhere.

Where I live now in southern Missouri, I don't have the sandy banks of the Delaware River a half block away, but resort areas are all around us — hills, valleys, woods — we can take a different drive every Sunday after church, of which there are an abundance to choose from.

We should be happy in America, especially in the Ozarks, my home for the past eight years.

97

I WILL BE 99 years old in July 2003. I have been asked frequently, "What have you learned from these many years of living? Most people your age are housebound at best." "What medication do you take?" "Are times better or worse?" etc.

I would not express my thoughts on these subjects if I had not been asked to do so.

To answer the first question, I will say, "Don't try to do everything at once — just keep moving, and sit down for five minutes between tasks. Be good to yourself."

As for the medication I take — just calcium every day and a popular pill for a tired back.

Anyone would say times are better today, but there are areas where improvements are in order.

Probably there have been more changes in the past century than in any previous century, or that will be in the next hundred years. No doubt, there have been more good changes than bad ones, but the latter ones are gaining by leaps and bounds, judging by almost every morning newspaper. I am happy with the environment we live in today, but if our inventors don't slow down trying to "make life easier" for us, we won't need to use our brains or hands at all.

Television is a great entertainer and teacher. I watch it some every day, but am very selective. I am glad I can wipe out the trash, the cruelty, etc., with the flip of a finger. It is a concern to watch children lolling around on the couch watching senseless programs, instead of playing or enjoying the outdoors, as we did in our youth.

Now, about some of the senseless programs such as some of the talk shows that adults watch, where three or more are trying to be heard at the same time, the result is that you can't understand any of the angry voices. That is a good time to interrupt with, "I think I smell smoke."

I enjoy being 98 years old. Why not enjoy myself as much as someone in the teens, middle age, or any age? Actually, the young people are in greater danger of extinction than I, for I don't drive any more, and when I ride with a group, I am usually in the back. There is something to be said for being in the back seat!

98

MY REASONS ARE many for writing this book — for my children and any interested readers.

I think we should all be happy. In America we are blessed in just being here — to me it is the best place on the globe. In the news, we see pictures of those who hope for nothing more than a bit of plain food and a little comfort. Some are worse off than the animals that can at least graze and find a puddle of unclean water which humans cannot ingest. Our intelligent, inventive people who have created more comfort for those already comfortable should work on a plan to assist the disadvantaged — not a solution perhaps, but at least an improvement.

It seems we don't need to find new worlds out there in space. Let's fix this one — here and there.

Among the "here and there" are morals. I have a newspaper clipping, yellow with age, that impressed me so much that I have put it with my keepers. I don't know the author of it, but the first paragraph is very "to the point." It stresses that moral standards will need to be changed if the "wrongs" in our lives today can be corrected. Neither politics nor economics can solve such problems. We do suffer from the "collapse" of the family, which is the stronghold of our lives. What once was a lifetime commitment is now "feel free to cancel at any time." The children suffer in divorce; when the bonds of home are broken, children don't feel safe and secure. Many look for a different lifestyle as they grow up. Sadly, a "nobody cares about me" attitude is what they assume. "They didn't even think of me when they split, so I won't ask them what I should strive for."

Since the abortion issue was a major one in the election year of 2000, I'll take advantage of the opportunity to say, "It is entirely up to the pregnant lady," her status quo, her health, her happiness, would the baby be better off having never had to face the family's problems? My opinion is, "Abortion is regrettable."

 99 

THE FOLLOWING ARE a collection of stories and poems I have written over the years when the inspiration forced my hand to paper. I have always enjoyed putting thoughts into a poem, whether humorous or contemplative. The short stories are taken from real incidents and have given many a reason to laugh, especially to those acquainted with the "subjects" who inspired them. I hope you, the reader, can glean some enjoyment from these reflections, too.

TUG-OF-WAR

(1943)

Although work for Defense is sweeping the nation
And efforts are made via radio station
To reach you and me — e'en the silent old whittler,
To tell us we must act at once to beat Hitler,
There is always somebody who stands up and shouts,
"Should we think just of trouble? Well, I have my doubts."

The fanciful one in our town is named Midge,
Who assembled a foursome to learn expert bridge.
She hired a teacher who knew about bidding,
When to play fair, and when to be "kidding,"
Who carefully dissected slamming and scoring
And never a minute was wasted or boring.
The spellbound attention of four eager women
Who hoped that their days of "taking a trimmin' "

Were over forever, because of the knowledge
That they would acquire attending "bridge college,"
Would last for an hour — maybe less, maybe more,
Then quick as a flash, they're discussing the war.

The cards are forgotten and so is the tutor,
And each lady confesses that things do not suit 'er.
"Our progress is slow — our methods are lacking.
We need bigger minds to give us more backing."
"More men should be drafted for training and such,
I'm telling you, we're dawdling too much."
"The money we're spending is simply outrageous
And yet, as you see by the daily front pages,
The enemy's forces continue to pound.
Looks like the Allies should be gaining ground."
This is the story of the group that I chose,
But it's only a sample, as everyone knows.

Now, many good people make up this great nation,
And a war such as this creates much sensation.
Opinions are voiced in every chance meeting.
We hardly take time to exchange friendly greeting
Before we embark on the subject of war —
What we think should be done and been done before.

What are we doing, depending on luck?
Expecting to win, but just "passing the buck"?
We're just watching the papers for final decisions,
Then starting at once to make some revisions.
It isn't the men in D.C. that are erring.
It's people like you and like me should be caring
Enough to take part in defending our nation
By accepting new rules without altercation.

Let's be patriotic and stop criticizing,
Stop finding fault and start harmonizing.
Let's have courage and faith, plus plenty of hope
And all start pulling the same end of the rope.

HAPPY, HAPPY BIRTHDAY

(Poem for Nancy, 1951)

We wanted to send you a piece of clothes,
But mercy, you have so many of those.
Camera, perfume, jewelry and such —
We didn't think you'd care for them much.

To get some ideas we covered each block
And fin'ly decided we'd give you a clock.
We were partic'lar in making a choice —
It's a "cuckoo" we wanted — one with a voice.

They had none — could get one — would order — but shucks,
They are imported — cost thirty-five bucks.
We couldn't afford that — but here's one that's nice,
'Twill serve the same purpose as one twice the price.

Just set it on mantel in very plain sight;
It serves as a hint for your callers at night.
When the hour is late, say, "Oh, mercy me — ah,"
Then look at the clock — he'll get the ide-ah.

We're all short of money and business is tough,
To buy four nice presents, we hadn't enough.
We pooled our resources. By the names you will see
That this gift is from Daddy, Jack, Sally and me.

PEACE

Each of us has an obligation
To protect this thing called Earth;
We may use it or abuse it,
Choice is ours from day of birth.

If I were given earth to tend
And had magic in my hands,
I'd clean the air, the sky, the seas,
Let sun shine on our lands.

I'd box the trash, the vice, the crime,
Of drugs leave not a trace.
"No place to put it," do you say?
Just blast into outer space!

If magic could be ours to use
And problems made to cease,
How proud and happy we would be,
We'd have a MASTER PEACE.

A REAL CHRISTMAS

Along about this time of year
I know the holidays are near;
I want so many lovely things,
From Christmas cards to pretty rings.

My list grows longer by the minute;
You'd be surprised at some things in it,
And then along with all the rest,
I want a party with formal dress.

Quick as a flash it comes to mind,
My Christmas spirit's the selfish kind;
I haven't thought of a single gift
To give to one who needs a lift.

I rush to my bank and count the pennies;
There are several nickels, even some "ten-ies";
I hurry to town for gifts and holly
To make my presents look real jolly!

And now that I sit beneath our tree,
So heavily decked with gifts for me,
I know that I've learned the secret of living —
It's not in the getting, but in the giving.

THESE BOYS

Some folks like to talk about clothes,
Some about school and some about shows,
Others prefer to talk in relation
To current problems facing our nation;
But no matter what topic the public enjoys,
I like to talk on the subject of "boys."

There are tall ones and short ones, lean ones and stout,
Dark ones and light ones, with curls and without;
When selecting a hair-do, they have many good lines,
For one day it bristles, the next day it shines.
But however they wear it, they always look nice;
It's diversification that gives life its spice.

Their fashions amaze me and I like them much better
Than the fashion for girls — a skirt and a sweater.
Now you know why we hurry right home after school —
It's to change to blue jeans and plaid shirt as a rule.

I really am jealous of those colorful vehicles
That the boys can revive with a few extra nickels.
Now my father won't let me drive our old machine,
But I hope to convince him by the time I'm sixteen.

Here are a few of the impressions I've had;
Most of them good, some almost bad.
But with all of their faults plus their racket and noise,
An exceedingly interesting subject — the boys!

A GUY NAMED NEIL

I know a young man who sets an example
For those other guys who are likely to trample
On thoughts of assisting with housewifely chores
Like cooking or cleaning — consider them bores.

He takes to the kitchen like bees take to honey,
Does a barbecued roast, be it cloudy or sunny.
He will diaper the baby or give him a bath
Or patch up his "hurt" with a hug and a laugh.

If you see some guy working with zip and with zeal,
Look once again, it's probably Neil.

MY TULIP BULB

My tulip bulb showed up today,
That perky little thing,
And 'though the North Wind said "Go 'way,"
She said, "Oh, no, it's spring!

"I've slept in long dark solitude
and dreamt of seeing light;
'Tween every dreamy interlude
I'd push with all my might.

"Now that I'm here, I want to grow;
I'm still a myster-ee.
If I don't grow, I'll never know
What color I would be!"

TRASH OR TREASURE

I left my home of sixty years
To re-locate as old age nears.
It's Springfield where I'll settle down;
It's such a fascinating town.

It's rife with signs of Christian lore
And scenic beauty's at my door.
But now I can't believe my eyes —
Can that be trash that flits and flies?

As daylight dawns, a sorry sight
To see what happened in the night —
Cor-ru-gated boxes thrown,
Cups and straws and butts wind-blown.

Candy wrappers, plastic sacks,
To be picked up by tired backs.
What's happened to our self-respect
When we allow such sad neglect?

Please join me as I raise my hand
To swear I'll beautify this land,
For people going through our town —
Like me — might choose to settle down.

GRÜNBACH

Nestling against a hillside
Rich in vineyards,
Grünbach, the changeless, slumbers.
An idyllic Swabian village,
So deep in its tranquility
That were Claus to awaken from centuries of sleep
In the graveyard,
He would find
His house unchanged,
Still lived in
By his descendants.
Generations have come,
Have gone,
Knowing no other sight
But that of the Swabian hillside.
Yet others have sought new lands
Which became the native land
Of their children
And children's children.
When the war of the nations
Tore the world asunder,
The sons of Claus arose
And under three banners
Followed their leaders.
There were they who fought
For the Fatherland,
Who died for their vine-clad hills.
Their names engraved
On the walls of the churchyard
Speak of their devotion.
There were they who heard
The call of the Czar
And left their fields
In the Ukraine
To battle their Grünbach brethren.

Still others crossed the sea
To a land unknown
To Claus and those of his time
To subdue their German kinsmen.
Claus would be amazed
At the numbers of his family
And at the miles and differences
Which separate them.
Yet I, from across the sea,
Standing at the graves of my kindred,
Gazing at the hills in the distance,
At the old, old vineyards,
Feel the changeless scene about me.
It seems I, too, am a part of Grünbach
And this peaceful Swabian countryside.

— *By Emma Knauer, my cousin*

CHRISTMAS DINNER, 1977

The first faux pas was made by me,
The failure of my recipe
For fudge I'd made for many a day
For Jim who oft was heard to say,
"Best fudge I ever ate."

The next reverse of well-made plans
Was made by dozens of demands
Of shoppers late at Shively's Store,
Causing us to leave at four
Instead of three.

Now Sally knows the road by heart,
But something flipped in her mental chart,
For we missed the turn she knows so well,
Trying to find the Carousel
At the mall.

Nancy had the dressing fixin's,
But I'm too old to use the mix and
So the dressing was a flop,
Even burned it on the top
Of the range.

It took strong hands/athletic muscles
With many pulls and yanks and tussles.
We should have had a rope or cable
To move that bird from range to table,
Spilled the gravy.

The 30-pounder was a dandy;
Jim with slicing knife was handy.
The gang with eyes and mouths wide open
For a sample were a hopin'
But the bird was rare.

Tried the turkey — couldn't risk it,
But Nancy filled the gap with brisket.
I said, "The extras you have not,
Just eat some more of what you've got."
MERRY CHRISTMAS!

MY HOUSE BY THE SIDE OF THE TRACK

There was one stipulation when buying a home,
Were it mansion or cottage or tar paper shack,
The size and the price and the style didn't matter
As long as 'twas far from the train and the track.

Such were our thoughts in the years of our past;
Howe'er were they started, one wonders?
For folks of all ages have thrilled to the train
As it whistles and wheezes and thunders.

I've wondered why people were riding the train;
Where were they going? Whom hoping to see?
I could see many faces — no doubt, many races,
And when I would wave, they'd wave back to me.

My little grandchild, impressed by the train,
Said, "You are so lucky — living so near,
If you didn't have so much housework to do,
You could count all the cars, each day of the year."

(The grandchild is Kristi.)

POSSUM'S REVIVAL

Our children were always encouraged to have compassion for all creatures, so it was not surprising that during their adolescent years we had the equivalent of a mini zoo, had they all appeared at the same time. Rabbits, turtles, pigeons, toads, fish, cats and dogs, and just about anything that was furred or feathered, skinned or scaled were our guests for various periods of time. One such creature is more memorable than all the rest and sort of climaxed our wildlife era. You see, we had never had a possum, as I called it. There could be opposition here, as I am most uninformed about small suburban wildlife.

It was on a very cold and drizzly evening after school that our 10-year-old son, Jack, greeted me with an especially cheerful, laughing, "Hi, Mom, guess what I found," and a mysterious bulge beneath his coat. He was so ecstatic over his find that I withheld my abhorrence when he set down that hideous, dirty, wet little thing on my kitchen floor. I quickly vetoed his plea for a box in his room. He compromised for a box in the back yard, with plenty of running room for the creature at the end of a small chain, the other end of which we fastened to a small tree. As night came, Jack reluctantly left his friend, whom I'll call simply "Possum," eager for morning and reunion with his new pet.

I was busy with the orange juice, cereal and milk when I heard the scream. "Mom, come quick, hurry. He's dead, he's dead. Make him breathe like you did Nancy's rabbit" (he had forgotten that we had held a full-scale funeral for the rabbit a few days after its revival).

Apparently, Possum had climbed the tree, crawled out onto

an icy branch and lost his footing, for there he hung by the chain, his fur covered with ice crystals and his body lifeless and stiff. Jack stood by, wrenching his hands, and between tears and hopeful giggles, begged me for a miracle.

We freed the little creature, put him on a pallet near a register in the kitchen and started massaging the little lung area, intermittently dropping a bit of warm water-whiskey mixture into its mouth. The cheers from watching your favorite team would have been challenged by the acclamation and laughter when my spectators saw the little nose start to twitch, then the paws jerk a bit, and finally the beady eyes opening. (May I interrupt here to say that if you have never revived a possum, you have missed something — the redolence from whatever perfume possums use to be attractive is utterly insufferable to humans.)

With breakfast forgotten and first-aid successfully completed, it was time to think of Possum's future. The family voted on whether he should be bond or free, and the latter prevailed. Jack agreed with a tearful, "I just want him to be happy." When the sun rose high and liberated the ice-covered grass and trees, we freed Possum to pursue his innate endeavors and live happily ever after, or as long as possums live, given a second chance.

MR. JAM-UP

No one seems to know how Mr. Jam-Up earned his nickname. Was he addicted to jam on his bread? Maybe he was always in a jam or a crush of people or circumstances? In his chosen career, perhaps he jammed the "merchandise" he handled with more vehemence than necessary? One could only conjecture, having no conclusive evidence, that his daddy was "James," and since there were so many Jimmies already, Jam-Up was the perfect moniker, serving two purposes — individuality and admission to the awkwardness of the growing boy. Be that as it may, he was unique, for who can recall knowing another Jam-Up?

On almost any weekday morning, when activity accelerated from snail's pace at six to haphazard helter-skelter at ten or so, the music of Jam-Up's old spring wagon's wheels hitting the bricks could be heard somewhere in town, for he had a bit of business just about everywhere. He sat high up on that old backless seat, but always hunched forward in deep thought, unaware of his disheveled shoulder-length hair, old oversized shirt and overalls, or even of the discredit due him for the slackness of the reins. All went well, however, for the aging but well-fed horse knew the route for every day of the week — when to stop and when to go. Mr. Jam-Up seemed to lean so far forward at times, it seemed he was dozing in an effort to finish his eight hours of sleep in a more pleasant environment than the modest quarters he called home.

Pity was unwelcome to this quiet, slow-stepped man. He asked no favors, his words were few, his business concluded on the spot, and he walked away from criticism, leaving further conversation impossible. His swarthy, furrowed face with its heavy-lidded eyes and his leathery and gnarled hands spoke of a lifetime devoid of luxury and sumptuousness. He was earning his living, owed no one, cared for his own in his fashion and asked only to be allowed a free lane on the streets to carry on his business. A state of peace and well-being surfaced through the appearance one got at first glance — that of a wasted life.

Mr. Jam-Up had a wonderful friend, always on the seat beside him, protecting, warning and adoring him. She followed wherever he led and asked only for food, shelter, love, and to be at his side. Another friend sat in the back, also asking little more than daily sustenance and to be allowed to ride along, with nothing between her and the rattling old boards of the wagon floor. She was the recipient of much sympathy from townsfolk for being sardined into a dirty little corner, with "merchandise" and worn-out wares all around her. Only the jerks of the vehicle, the stops-and-goes told her the progress they were making on the route, but she, too, asked for nothing more and looked forward only to the next day, which would vary little, if any.

Careers, professions and vocations are varied and many. Luckily, there are varied and numerous aspirants to most opportunities, but no applicant could fill the vacancy left by Mr. Jam-Up, "Warrensburg's Trash Pick-Up" of the 1930s, whose faithful dog sat on the seat beside him and whose constant wife bounced around on the floor in the back.

IS MY HOME MY CASTLE?

It is spring again and time once more to hold a conference with myself and my house, which really does seem to speak to me at times. For several years now, self-appointed advisors have offered hints and innuendos as to the advisability of selling my house, all of which really adds up to their hint that I am getting too old to know what is best for me. To this I simply reply, "I know what you are saying, but I am not old — just middle-aged." They tell me I don't need this big house or that 150-foot deep backyard to tend.

In fact, they say I should be in a first floor apartment to avoid steps. Ironically, another will say I should be on the second or third floor to discourage thieves who might have difficulty and give up trying to move my furniture down one or two flights of steps. Also, I should be within walking distance of the post office, grocery store and church. They don't say what I should do about getting to my hairdresser, my job as volunteer Red Cross assistant at Johnson Memorial, my visits to Manor Nursing Home, my bridge clubs or my bowling league. I caught myself looking at a new car the other day. What would I do with a new car if I walked wherever I went? And what would I do for exercise at home if I could no longer run from the backyard when the telephone rings? "Friends, I'll shelve your help and take a new survey of my house — the pros and cons of relocating."

As I step outside, I am imagining what the various adjuncts of the house proper would be telling me if they could. The garage could rebuke me something like this: "Don't tear me down now. Remember all those times you wished I was wider for those big cars that appeared after World War II?

Now that cars are smaller than ever before, use me. All I need is a new door with a Genie."

As I near the backyard, the clothesline and poles are threatening to fight back if necessary and saying, "Remember how your husband had concrete blocks buried deeply for us iron poles? Why, one day some excavators like Carnaven and Carter may think those blocks lead to another King Tut's Tomb. Besides, don't I take over when the electricity fails?"

The woodpile by the barbeque oven is complaining about unrequited love. "Haven't I taken care of you the last two winters after the storm blew down your tree? No adolescent little new house on a bare lot, like you want, would furnish such good wood, free of charge!"

That dignified voice I hear might be that of my stately linden tree saying, "Remember how I came here from Philadelphia?" And I would have to say, "Yes, I remember bringing you, a tiny twig, with barely any roots, wrapped in soaked swaddling something or other, and placing you in a plastic cover and putting you into my suitcase. Your parents are still in Philadelphia, and your grandparents are in Stuttgart, Germany. How we cared for you — fenced you in to avoid those predators, the rabbits and lawn mowers, and careless feet. Then we wrapped you carefully against Missouri's vicious winters. Finally you grew, and now you are taller than my two-story house. There are not many of you, so I should guard you well."

Looking at me now with disdainment is my white board fence, the arbitrator years ago, I suppose, in a property line dispute. It is saying, "The neighbor's boys are almost grown now and not likely to jump across for a ball or a Frisbee any more. Just give me a new board or two and a coat of paint, and let me stay."

On my front lawn now, I can almost hear a chuckle from my big blue spruce that has been considered "too big" for many years. It has caught up with the telephone wires many times, but each time it touches the wires, those dear boys from the telephone company approach me. I apologize for my monstrosity, they accept it and add on another extension to the top of the pole with, "We don't want you to lose that tree."

Then there is the lumpy brick street apparently laid by a jittery bricklayer years ago. One questions the sobriety of the driver as one watches him trying to miss all the highs and lows in the street. I just pretend I'm in old Boston where every brick street is precious and loved.

How many times I have heard, "Joanne, you have the most difficult driveway. It is impossible to make it in one attempt." But I have made it the first time in spite of seven obstacles, which must be a record for driveways. There is the retaining wall, the telephone pole, the "No Parking" sign, the trespassing tree branches from the spruce which has priority, cars parked on opposite side of the street, children on the sidewalk with bicycles and tricycles, and the traffic to and from the high school. In 39 years, I've missed them all.

So I think I've won the argument for another year, for all the objects of criticism seem to be saying, "Like you, we are not old — just middle-aged."

THE DREAD OF CHRISTMAS

There is a saying to the effect that there is something good and something not so good about everything. In the Christian world it is almost impossible to find anything but beauty and goodness in commemoration of the greatest gift ever given, the birth of Jesus Christ. This event was the inception of the Christmas celebration each year on the 25th day of December.

St. Nicholas, patron saint of children, continued the spirit of giving in an acceptable manner by distributing gifts and food to the children, the poor and the sailors whose livelihood and very existence depended on their wrestle with the sea. No doubt the real meaning of giving was still alive when parents observed the custom with gifts for their children — sweet meats, trinkets, tiny home-made toys or needed mittens and scarves. Later, in adulthood, natural reciprocation by the children still held to the main objective, the desire to show love and appreciation and experience the pleasure of giving which their parents taught them is more blessed than receiving.

As our world progressed and machines started making things faster than hands ever could, people became affluent and competitive, and the real spirit of Christmas started fading, until today many a child who is asked what Christmas represents will say, "It is the day we get lots of presents." To merchants, it is the time of year the cash register rings most frequently. To the social circles, Christmas through New Year's is a time of parties, dances and over-imbibing. For as long as 31 days, expensive energy is squandered to find who can use the most colored lights in the house, yard, lamp post, and even the garage and barn, when a tiny candle in the window would thrill the passersby even more.

100

THIS FINAL CHAPTER may not be interesting to the average reader, but will mean much to the family. It is made up of the arrival of my nine grandchildren, the first in 1958, and the last in 1966, with seven more between the first and last. Here is a very brief description of each one of these beautiful children.

1. Sally's Dana Ellen arrived to brighten our lives and she has been doing it ever since, forty-odd years. She finds that proverbial light at the end of the tunnel quicker than most of us do, and is usually wearing a smile.

2. Daughter Nancy gave us Julie Ann in 1959; she has been an exemplary granddaughter to me and a friend to all she meets. She never misses an occasion to send a card, letter, even a gift.

3. Our next blessing was Kristi Lynn, whom Marilyn and Bill adopted in 1960. She was as dear to our hearts as any child could be.

4. Sally had our first grandson, Robert, in January 1961. He has been very close to me, especially in later years, when I welcomed a helping hand, and now a supporting arm.

5. Bill and Marilyn had Carrie Ellen in 1962. She doesn't keep up very well, but she is married now, living in Con-

necticut. I am sure she would be glad to see all of us.

6. Nancy's Nicholas came in 1962, also; it was time for another boy, so we were glad he evened the score — almost.

7. We skipped 1963. In 1964, Leslie Reneé arrived at Nancy's. She inherited my love for travel. Several years back, we did a bit of it together — a journey to Europe.

8. The next three years were happy ones for son Jack. He met Mary Lu Stundebeck at CMSC — they married in 1964 in her hometown of Salisbury, Missouri. They became parents of Jason (John) in 1965, and Clayton in 1966. I know no one has perfect children, but Jason and Clay are as near the top as one can get in this world. Today, they are handsome young men, great fathers, and put me, the grandmother, on a higher plateau than I deserve.

All of our nine grandchildren fit easily into a decade with a year to spare, so they all know each other well, visit each other — sort of grew up together. Ideal, I think.

The weddings of our grandchildren were scattered all over — every one interesting.

Dana married Don Duncan in a quaint little country church near Nixa — very impressive and sincere.

Robert married Lestine Duncan in a beautiful ceremony in a hosta-filled cavern near their home in Ozark, Missouri.

Julie and Neil Foth married in a garden wedding in Santa Fe, New Mexico — very nice, with many attendants from the Midwest.

Nicholas and Candy Crouch married in the "Wilderness Church" in Silver Dollar City near Branson, Missouri. A unique wedding in a memorable old church.

Reneé and Kurt Lichtman married in New York City — music, flowers and food in abundance!

Kristi married in Florida — surprised us — husband is Robert Pape. They live in Jacksonville.

Carrie married in Hawaii — lives in Connecticut.

Jason married Whitney Harrison in a beautiful Methodist Church ceremony in Wichita, Kansas.

Clayton married Jennifer Thomas in a Catholic Church in Wichita. Another memorable occasion.

As of June 2003, there are now 14 great-grandchildren. They arrived in this order: Jeanelle, Lee, Kim, Robbie Jr., Jackson, Summer, Gabriel, Harrison, Chloe, Spencer, Paulina, Gracie, Carson and Elise.